BLOODY
HISTORY
of LONDON

BLOODY HISTORY *of* LONDON
Crime, Corruption and Murder

John D. Wright

amber
BOOKS

Published by
Amber Books Ltd
74–77 White Lion Street
London
N1 9PF
United Kingdom
www.amberbooks.co.uk
Appstore: itunes.com/apps/amberbooksltd
Facebook: www.facebook.com/amberbooks
Twitter: @amberbooks

ISBN: 978-1-78274-496-2

Editor: Sarah Uttridge
Designer: Zoe Mellors
Picture research: Terry Forshaw

Manufactured in China

CONTENTS

INTRODUCTION

The long life of London Town has been one of pride and pain. Its citizens have seen conquerors come and go, and watched their city become the centre of a global Empire. Behind the glory, however, was a hidden history of blood and gore.

F EW OF THE world's great cities have equalled the beauty and power of London. The capital of the United Kingdom has been a centre of culture, commerce, industry and finance for most of its extraordinary history. Growing from a Roman settlement to become the heart of the largest Empire on Earth, this dynamic city has remained an inspiration for Kings and commoners alike. 'When you're tired of London,' the writer and wit Samuel Johnson famously said, 'you're tired of life.'

London life, however, was often brutal, violent and short. During its 2000 years, Londoners have suffered plagues, fires, riots, revolutions and countless murders. Death has come in many ways, from Royal executions by axe, stake and rope to serial killings in dark back streets to modern murder by radioactive poison and terrorist attacks.

Scandal was also never far away in the city's history. The Restoration of 1660 ushered in a merry debauchery. Insider trading brought about the South

OPPOSITE: **Life was always bleak and short in the early years of London and England, but the native population suffered the most from invaders, especially the violence of the Romans and extreme brutality of the Vikings.**

ABOVE: Organized medieval combat was used to settle differences and win awards at games. Anglo-Norman law also used trial by arms to determine innocence or guilt, with some suspects allowed to nominate others to fight for them.

Sea Bubble, whose crash ruined many in 1720. Celebrated figures caught in sin included the future Edward VII in 1868, playwright Oscar Wilde in 1895 and John Profumo, Secretary of State for War, in 1963 as Londoners enjoyed the 'Swinging 60s.'

Early Warfare

Recorded violence began with the Roman invasion in 43AD that routed local tribes. Resistance became fierce under Boudica, Queen of the Iceni tribe, but her revolt came to a bloody end in the year 61. Later uprisings were quickly defeated before the Romans departed by 410AD. Tribes struggled for power and then had to withstand a Viking assault in the ninth century.

London would fall again in 1066 when William the Conqueror defeated the English force and was ordained King on Christmas Day in the city.

The Cruelty of the Crown

British sovereigns brought wealth and acclaim to London, but ruled with deadly powers. The medieval city saw Henry II order the assassination in 1170 of Thomas Becket, the Archbishop of Canterbury, and Richard III apparently had his two young nephews murdered in 1483 at the Tower of London, known for its torture. In the sixteenth century, Henry VIII became England's most infamous King by ordering two of his six wives to be beheaded in the Tower.

Not all of the brutal rulers were Kings. Mary Tudor became known as 'Bloody Mary' after having the Nine-Day Queen, Lady Jane Grey, beheaded in 1554. Then as Mary I, she ordered the deaths of some 280 non-Catholics, who were burned at the stake, including the Archbishop of Canterbury.

This murderous rule came to an end in 1649 with the public beheading of Charles I. But Londoners themselves faced even more death two decades later when the Great Plague struck down some 60,000 people and the Great Fire raged for four days, leaving barely one-fifth of the city standing.

Murder Most Foul

As violent as their rulers could be, average Londoners have faced greater danger from their peers. The horrendous murders of 'Jack the Ripper' in 1888 highlighted the danger waiting for them on the city streets, as did the deaths of Bulgarian dissident Georgi Markov, stabbed in the leg with a poison-tipped umbrella on Waterloo Bridge in 1978, and Roberto Calvi, 'God's Banker' for the Vatican, found murdered and hanging from Blackfriars Bridge in 1982.

Riots have also occurred throughout history, from the Massacre of Jews at the coronation of Richard I in 1189 and the Gordon Riots against Catholics in 1780, to those against police in working-class areas in 1985 and 2011. In between were the large Poll Tax riots in Central London in 1990.

More blood, however, has been spilled in London's homes. Notorious examples include Doctor Crippen and Lord Lucan. Hawley Crippen, an American homeopath and medicine dispenser, poisoned and murdered his wife and fled with his lover to Canada. He was arrested there in 1910 to become the first man caught by a telegraph message. Lord Lucan, an earl, is said to have killed his children's nanny, mistaking her for his wife. He disappeared, supposedly with help from wealthy friends, and has never been tracked down, despite various reported sightings.

Policing London

Keeping up with criminals was never easy in the city's early life, a task eventually headed by Roman legionnaires. Justice was severe, including beheading and crucifixion, but convictions usually relied on unfounded suspicions, eyewitness accounts and often torture. This resulted in executions of far too many innocent people in Londinium.

Only in 1829 did London have a standard police organization. Sir Robert Peel founded the Metropolitan Police Force that year, and members of the force were called 'bobbies' after him. Among other things, he ended the savage death penalties that were often handed out for minor crimes, such as stealing food. The headquarters were located at Scotland Yard, and this police presence was just in time for the bloody Victorian crimes that were made more frightening by the growing popular press. The height of fear was reached when a killer murdered and disembowelled five victims in East London, leading newspapers to splash 'Jack the Ripper' stories across their front pages.

Peel may have created a modern police force, but it still often relied on guesswork. Science came to the rescue in the late nineteenth century. Photography was used to document crime scenes in the 1860s and fingerprinting began to catch criminals in the 1880s. Modern DNA evidence came into being a century later, and today's DNA databases give London's police an upper hand in fighting local and international crime.

The Scull Cap

The Collar

Weighing 12 pounds.

Weighing 15 pounds.

Weighing 40 pounds.

(e) The Sheers

Weighing 20 pounds.

b. Skull-Cap ; *c.* Collar ; *d.* Heavy Fetters ; *e.* Sheers.

THE CRUELTIES IN THE MARSHALSEA PRISON

LEFT: Tortuous iron instruments were used on prisoners at London's infamous Marshalsea Prison in Southwark. Among the inmates were local criminals, pirates, dissenters and debtors, including Charles Dickens' father.

BELOW: A convenient way to solve overcrowded prisons and reduce crime was to ship criminals out of the country. A sentence of transportation sent the offender to America or Australia for years of hard labour, and few returned.

THE ANCIENT CITY

The Roman city of Londinium lived on the edge of chaos, forever a potential victim of local tribes intent on wrecking the foreign civilization that was ruling their land and threatening their culture, religion and values.

BEFORE THE ROMANS arrived, London did not exist. Archaeologists have uncovered small prehistoric settlements here and there along that stretch of the River Thames that flowed lower in those days. Celtic tribes, such as the Belgic from northern Gaul, commanded most of the southeastern land. Their farmsteads were successful and protected by a warrior class, but they were no match for the organized Roman legions.

The site for Londinium was selected by the Romans in the first century AD. It consisted of governmental, merchant and private buildings, a port and a military base from which legions were dispatched to subdue troublesome tribes. A future emperor, Vespasian, commanded the 2nd legion Augusta that won victories along the Thames and in the south. In the year 61, however, Londinium was sacked by the warrior Queen, Boudica, when the city's legions were putting down discontent in northern Wales. They returned to end the revolt and London would enjoy years of peace until the Romans' permanent withdrawal in

OPPOSITE: Reminders of the small town of Londinium are still around today, such as the boundaries of the City of London financial district, street names and layouts, and names derived from Roman gates, like Ludgate and Moorgate.

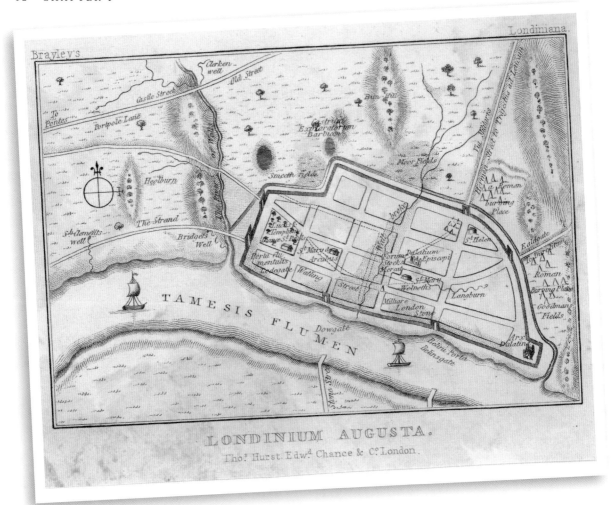

LONDINIUM AUGUSTA.

Tho.ᵖ Hurst. Edw.ᵈ Chance & Cᵒ London.

ABOVE: Beginning about the year 368, Londinium was called Augusta by officials who wanted it recognized as an imperial provincial capital. Within 40 years, however, the legions began to withdraw to put down troubles in Rome.

the sixth century to handle political crises at home. Left to fend for themselves, Londoners oversaw the decline and influence of their city, which became an Anglo-Saxon settlement. By the seventh century, it had grown in importance with expanded trade, but another occupation was on its doorstep from a more fearful invader: the Vikings.

Chaos and Conquest

When Julius Caesar and his legions landed in what is now Britain, they found the countryside occupied by an untidy collection of some 20 tribes who offered fruitless resistance to the powerful invaders. Caesar conquered the Catuvellauni tribe's army in 54BC and the British isle became a province of his Roman Empire. These impressive raids established no settlement at present-day London, and it would be up to Claudius to successfully invade in 43AD with about 40,000 men and establish bases at Londinium and Camulodunum (now Colchester). The settlement at London began to take on a permanent appearance, with a basilica, forum and bridge over the river. The legions were able to suppress most tribes and convince others to support their rule. This ended the Catuvellauni's dominance over rivals in the chaotic tribal landscape.

The Emperor's Elephants

The Emperor Claudius invaded England in 43AD, bringing along a corps of several elephants – estimates range from 12 to 38 – to impress and frighten the tribes. They sailed across the English Channel and apparently passed through the area of the future Londinium, crossing its river, and then helped demonstrate the power of Rome as a spectacular part of Claudius' triumphant entrance into Camulodunum. The Greco-Roman writer Polyaenus gave an account in the second century of local defenders fleeing in the face of one elephant that wore armour and carried archers (although Polyaenus mistakenly says the emperor was Caesar). Claudius left for home after a couple of weeks and took the elephants with him.

Boudica

Boudica, the warrior Queen of the Celtic Iceni tribe, had no intention of going gently into the Roman night. She had seen the kingdom of her husband, who ruled with Roman backing, plundered and annexed after his death around 60AD,

BELOW: Roman invasions were opposed by local tribes whose ferocious fighting abilities were no match for the superior weapons, armour, organization and training of the legions. Many tribes eventually chose peace as the best option.

RIGHT: Boudica matched Roman brutality with even more cruelty, using fire and torture. Tribes that had once been enemies joined her forces, convinced this splendid Queen was the one great chance to rid their country of the foreigners.

although he had divided his wealth with his family and the Emperor Nero. When Boudica tried to resist, she was stripped and flogged, her two daughters raped and her relatives became slaves.

Boudica's humiliation established her hatred for the Romans, and in the year 61 she went on a rampage, leading an army of 20,000 Celts that sacked and torched London, Colchester and other towns. The Roman Governor Suetonius Paulinus had initially decided to abandon London because the Celtic force was too large. Instead, he escorted residents who wished to leave the city that had no protective walls. Those who stayed were cruelly slaughtered.

Throughout the land, Boudica's soldiers wiped out entire civilian populations and levelled every house. Her forces, which included other tribes from East Anglia, massacred about 70,000 Romans and Britons without taking prisoners, preferring to hang, burn or even crucify them. Noble women were

WHO WERE THE ICENI?

The Iceni were a Celtic tribe that originated in the Iron Age and occupied what is now Norfolk and Suffolk in the East of England. They lived mostly in agricultural communities where they produced abundant handmade pottery and traded wool, managing sheep as well as cattle and horses.

The tribe was not poor. When the Romans landed under Claudius in 43ad, the Iceni were already producing gold and silver coins. They agreed a treaty with the invaders, but four years later rebelled after being ordered to disarm. The Romans put down this brief revolt and allowed Prasutagus, the husband of Boudica, to rule as a client King. After his death and Boudica's failed uprising, the Romans built the Iceni a new town near present-day Norwich to maintain the peace, but they were not urban people. The Iceni never revived their great kingdom and became an insignificant tribe.

selected to be impaled on spikes, with their breasts cut off and sewn into their mouths. Boudica's men also badly defeated Rome's 9th legion that marched as reinforcements from Lincoln.

The revolt ended badly for the Queen. Suetonius assembled a well-organized army that crushed Boudica's larger forces, probably in the Midlands, using javelins, arrows and swords to kill some 80,000 Celts while losing only 400 of his soldiers. The Queen with her daughters had driven a chariot among her troops. 'On this spot we must either conquer, or die with glory,' she said. 'There is no alternative. Though a woman, my resolution is fixed.' Her fate is uncertain: some accounts say she drank poison, some that she died of battlefield injuries or an illness, but others reported that she had escaped.

'Boudica's soldiers wiped out entire civilian populations and levelled every house.'

Bridging the Thames

The Romans' first London bridge was built in 52AD as a temporary structure, probably a pontoon construction with planks on boats, used to move legions over the land in order to subdue hostile tribes. It was only yards from the present London Bridge. The Thames at that time was wider and shallower. The bridge was rebuilt with timber about the year 55 and guarded by soldiers. Boudica's rampaging troops no doubt burned the bridge along with the city in the year 61, but it was rebuilt around 80AD, connecting the settlement at Southwark with the northern bank where Londinium rose to become a main Roman centre. The last Roman bridge in 300 led to the gateway in the city's wall. In 984AD, after Rome had withdrawn, records show the wooden bridge that existed then was used to execute a suspected witch by drowning.

THE WARRIOR QUEEN

Boudica was a flame-haired, very tall Celtic woman whose name in Celtic means 'Victory.' She was in her 30s when she was flogged for disputing the breakup of her husband's kingdom. Known for her intelligence, she had a harsh voice and piercing, fierce gaze. Her loose hair fell to her hips. She normally wore a multicoloured tunic and mantle fastened with a brooch; a decorative golden band known as a torc was worn tightly around her neck, the type worn by Celtic warriors who vowed to fight to the death. When speaking encouragement to her people, she would hold a spear. A bronze statue of Boudica and her daughters, dedicated in 1902 next to Westminster Bridge in London, shows her in a war chariot and grasping a spear.

RIGHT: The sculptor of the Boudica statue was Thomas Thornycroft, who also sculpted the 'Commerce' figures for London's Albert Memorial.

'The Roman's first London bridge was built in 52AD as a temporary structure.'

By the year 300, the Romans had added a wall around Londinium and spanned the Thames with a bridge leading to one of the city gates. These defences, however, were useless against internal power struggles within the city.

The Fires of Verulamium

The Roman town of Verulamium (now St Albans in Hertfordshire) was three times devastated by fire. Boudica sacked and burned it down in 61, although few real Roman buildings existed. Within a few years the town recovered to become a main centre for trade protected by a wall and ditch. The next destruction was not from an attack, but by accidental fire in the summer of 155AD. This was followed a century later by yet another devastating conflagration in 250AD. The buildings were small houses and shops constructed of clay and wood. Romans and Britons again rebuilt Verulamium, this time in stone with more space between the structures. It continued to grow as an important base for Roman power, commerce and culture, lying within a short trip to Londinium for both business and pleasure.

'One would think Romans in London saw enough violence in their daily lives.'

BELOW: The Roman Theatre of Verulamium was built around 140AD and eventually could seat some 2000 spectators. It was a theatre with a stage instead of an amphitheatre and was used for everything from religious events to wild beast shows.

Death in the Amphitheatre

One would think Romans in London saw enough violence in their daily lives, but they also enjoyed it for entertainment. Their amphitheatre in the middle of the city drew capacity crowds to watch the death battles of gladiators, the execution of criminals and prisoners of war, and brutal fights between wild animals released through a sliding trap door.

Workers discovered the amphitheatre in 1985 under the Guildhall Yard, a space originally within the Roman walls. Also found were 39 mutilated skulls,

which the Museum of London has dated between 120 and 160AD. They belonged to men in their 20s and 30s who had been decapitated, the mortal blow of mercy given to defeated gladiators. Prisoners condemned to death might also be given swords to kill one another in the arena.

The amphitheatre was first constructed of wood in 70AD and later rebuilt in stone and inlaid marble around 120AD to seat more than 7000 people on benches in the open air. Sand and gravel covered the floor of the fighting arena to soak up blood. The remains of the amphitheatre can now be viewed under the Guildhall Art Gallery.

The Roman Wall

Around the year 200 the Romans constructed a massive wall to protect London, probably from an invasion from the fearsome Celtic tribal confederation known as the Picts. The wall stretched some 4km (2.5 miles) and enclosed an area of about 134 hectares (330 acres) accessed by four city gates. In places it was 5.4m (18ft) high and 2.7m (9ft) thick. Incorporated in the wall was a Roman fort built a century earlier and housing 1000 members of the official guard of the Governor

ABOVE: Admission is free to the Roman Amphitheatre in the Guildhall Art Gallery, located off Gresham Street. The gallery also contains a range of paintings that capture the different stages of London's history.

of Britain. In 255AD, the wall was extended along the river to completely enclose the city and thwart any attacks by ships and other craft. Towers were added on the eastern section in the fourth century to increase protection.

After the Roman army left London, parts of the wall became weak and were repaired by the Anglo-Saxons. During the medieval era, long sections were used as part of the city's defence. A surviving section of the wall can now be seen on Tower Hill north of the Tower of London.

The Roman Citizens' Watch

Soldiers stationed during the early years of Londinium were responsible for enforcing the city's law and keeping order, but citizens often had to protect themselves from criminals who struck quickly and faded into the dark streets. Residents banded together to watch over houses and placed iron bars on their windows and heavy locks on doors. They also sought divine intervention, writing to their gods on lead tablets for help to bring justice to those who had injured them or stolen their property. To increase the chances of revenge, they added curses on the felons.

London's First Brothels

Known as lupanaria, the city's brothels originated when female slaves from other parts of the Roman Empire were shipped to Londinium for the pleasure of the occupying troops. The brothels were cheap houses on the south bank of the Thames that were run by local madams. The prostitutes were unpaid slaves and seldom lived beyond the age of 30. Local women could become prostitutes in the establishments by applying to a public health official. Legal brothels were carefully controlled with licences issued to prostitutes who were not slaves, being paid for their services and taxed by the government. The higher-born prostitutes would issue 'menus' listing what services were offered and provide a client with a token depicting his favourite predilection. One of these bronze tokens, slightly smaller than a 10 pence coin, was discovered in 2012 in mud near Putney Bridge.

All prostitutes were required to undergo regular inspections for venereal diseases. They faced serious competition from unregulated prostitutes who met clients for public sex in parks, gardens and even cemeteries, as well as during festivals, celebrations and sporting events.

Murder and Looting

By 284AD or so, Roman power was becoming unstable in Britain, with Franks and Saxons moving more or less freely to ravage the countryside. The Romans dispatched a powerful naval fleet, Classis Britannica, under the command of Carausius to restore order, but he joined with the invaders and took over control of Rome's army and navy in Britain, declaring himself Emperor and ruling from 287 to 293AD.

This ended abruptly when Carausius was assassinated in York by his own admiral and finance minister, Allectus, who took the imperial title. His rule was

OPPOSITE: The wall of Londinium was one of the Romans' largest building projects in Britain. They used about 85,000 tons of Kentish ragstone in the construction. The wall determined the shape of the city for 1600 years.

'The prostitutes were unpaid slaves and seldom lived beyond the age of 30.'

ABOVE: Romans brought their coinage with them to Britain, and new coins were minted by emperors and would-be emperors. Local tribes had produced their own coins, but eventually adopted the better regulated and versatile Roman ones.

even shorter, after a Roman army under Constantius Chlorus (the future Emperor Constantius I) arrived in 296AD with a plan for a divided attack. Constantius would take a fleet to London and send a force under Asclepiodotus to land on the coast of Sussex. Fog let him avoid Allectus' waiting fleet, but forced the ships to turn back from Londinium. Allectus marched his men, mostly Franks and Saxons, out of the city to confront Asclepiodotus, losing both the battle and his life. The remnants of the defeated army fled into Londinium to murder residents and loot the many riches held in the city. This was short-lived, however, as favourable winds brought Constantius' fleet up the river to save Londinium, fighting through the streets until the enemy was slain. A gold medallion was soon struck with his image and the inscription calling him 'the restorer of eternal light.' The reverse side depicts Constantius on horseback being welcomed at the city gate by a female personifying Londinium while his warship rides on the Thames.

'They were tortured in the worst ways imaginable before being beheaded.'

BELOW: Constans was the Roman Emperor from 337 to 350AD. In 340AD, his army defeated that of his brother, Constantine II, who then ruled Britain, and Constans would become the last legitimate Emperor to visit Britain.

Paulus 'The Chain'

The Emperor Constans visited London and Britain in 347AD, probably to rally troops and remind them that he was watching their situation. Three years after his return to Rome, Constans was assassinated by Magnentius, a native Briton who was one of his officers. Such a horror demanded revenge on those in Britain who might have been involved or even approved of the murder. Rome reached into its Empire to choose Paulus Catena, a Spanish notary known for his cruelty and sent him in 353AD to exact retribution.

Paulus had earned his surname of Catena ('The Chain') for his habit of placing heavy shackles on his prisoners and dragging them through the streets. His tortures and executions were so cruel in Britain that its civil ruler, Martin, made an effort to help the victims. Paulus accused him and several of his authorities of supporting the assassination. An effort by Martin and companions to kill Paulus failed, so Martin committed suicide with his own sword. When Paulus returned to Rome, he brought along many prisoners wrapped in chains. They were tortured in the worst ways imaginable before being beheaded. The more lucky victims were exiled.

Roman Burials

The Romans brought an advanced civilization to London and Britain, but part of it could be primitive when it came to death. Infanticide, usually by exposure, was practiced for children with physical problems or even those that were unwanted, which was often baby girls. Emperor Valentinian had issued an edict against this in 374AD, but made exceptions for poor families. Roman rule also was unable to stop the local primitive practice of human sacrifice involving ritual killings.

Roman burials were normally done with great respect, but bodies have been discovered bound, dismembered, decapitated and mutilated. Some were buried face down with stones placed on their backs, perhaps a sign that they were buried alive. The magazine *British Archaeology* noted that in London's Eastern Cemetery 14 bodies were buried in this manner, including a woman with her hands bound behind her back. At Spitalfields Roman Cemetery, a number of children have been found in this position, possibly because they were not baptized.

ABOVE: Archaeologists have excavated Roman cemeteries in London. They are discovered under land where new buildings are constructed. Bodies from this cemetery in Aldgate have been moved, and the graves show how closely together they were buried.

Roman Rule Ends

In 367AD, the Picts joined with the Irish (Scoti) to rampage violently through the country and into London, which they plundered until driven back in 369AD by Theodosius. Roman troops began to be withdrawn in 383AD, and Germanic raiders began to attack the southern and eastern coasts. Rome itself was being invaded, and in 409AD when Britain asked the Emperor Flavius Honorius for troops, he advised them to take care of the problem themselves. Roman rule ended the following year when Honorius released the city and other English towns from their allegiance. Londinium began a long decline and in the late fifth century was a virtual uninhabited ruin.

England's First Christian Martyr

The story of St Alban is clouded by the mists of history. Alban was said to be an English pagan who lived in Verulamium (near today's St Albans in Hertfordshire) or sometimes Londinium. He served in the Roman army when Christians

were being persecuted. Alban gave secret shelter to a Christian priest named Amphibalus who converted him during their time together. When authorities tracked the priest to his door, Alban exchanged clothes with Amphibalus and the man escaped. Alban was arrested, and a long trial was held. He refused to recant his new faith and was scourged and given the death sentence the priest would have received. He was beheaded sometime between 209 and 304AD. Amphibalus was also soon arrested nearby and martyred.

Alban's martyrdom was immediately commemorated at the spot where he was killed with a shrine. This was later replaced in 792AD by Saint Albans Abbey, which in turn became a cathedral in 1877. Pilgrims continue to pray there and St Albans Day is celebrated on 22 June by Catholics and 17 June by the Church of England. The town of St Albans grew up around the abbey.

The 'Great Slaughter'

Roman rule lasted for a fifth of London's total history. After the Romans left, the city declined, but was renewed as a centre of trade and of Christianity following the arrival of St Augustine in 597AD. Little was recorded about the growing city for nearly 200 years as Anglo-Saxons settled or forced their way among a population that had enjoyed peace and retained many Roman ideals.

This calm came to a shattering end in the eighth century when Viking raids swept the coasts. As the vicious Norsemen moved inland, London braced for the brutality depicted by survivors. The city's tragic turn came in 842AD with a Viking raid described by a historian as the 'great slaughter.' Another attack in 851AD saw Vikings sail up the river in 350 longboats to plunder and burn the city. Less damage occurred 20 years later when a Viking army made winter camp

OPPOSITE: St. Albans Cathedral stands on the oldest site of continuous Christian worship in Britain. In 2015 it celebrated the 900th anniversary of the completion of the Norman abbey in 1115, adding new statues of martyrs.

'Little was recorded about the growing city for nearly 200 years.'

BELOW: The Viking leader Olaf Tryggvason led raids on England in 991AD and 994AD, as depicted here. Both attacks resulted in England's King Ethelred II paying large sums in tribute. Tryggvason became Norway's King in 995AD.

THE SAVAGERY OF VIKINGS

Their name in Old Norse means 'pirate', and the Vikings lived up to that name and more. Mass murder and other atrocities were committed during their invasions of isolated communities and peaceful cities. One can imagine the fear of Londoners when news came in 793AD of the Norsemen's attack on Lindisfarne Priory on the northeast coast. In this remote spot they brutally murdered monks, stamped on their bodies and poured their blood around the altar, drowned some in the sea and carried off others in chains, including young apprentices.

A gruesome ritual of Viking execution was called 'the blood-eagle', in which an eagle was carved on the victim's back. This involved stabbing a man through the spine to sever his ribs, rip out the lungs and drape them over his shoulders to resemble an eagle's wings. Other accounts mention mass beheadings, babies tossed on spearheads and rape. Those allowed to survive were chosen as slaves for labour and prostitution. When their masters died, they were often beheaded and buried next to them.

ABOVE: Vikings showed no respect or fear of other religions, as seen in their attack on Lindisfarne, known as the Holy Island.

within London's old Roman walls. King Alfred of Wessex fought the invaders to a standstill in the countryside and occupied London in 886AD, repairing its defences. He turned it over to his son-in-law, Ethelred, who made it a key city opposing the Vikings. Sweyn Forkbeard (960–1014) would renew assaults on the city in 996AD and 1013. His son, Canute, captured London in 1016 by digging a ditch around London Bridge for his ships to attack. After securing England, his coronation led to safer times and ended the Viking threat. His stepson, Edward the Confessor, brought back English rule when crowned King in 1042 and built Westminster Abbey.

Pulling Down London Bridge

With Sweyn Forkbeard temporarily occupying London in 1014, Ethelred the Unready fled, but Sweyn soon died. Ethelred determined to retake the city from the remaining Danish troops, and received help from his ally, Olaf Haraldsson, the future King of Norway. The Danes were protected by a castle on the north side and a defensive work for troops in Sudvirke (Southwark).

According to Nordic legend, the enemy armed with spears took their position behind barricades on London Bridge to thwart any approaching ships. Ethelred and the other leaders with him decided to move their warships under the bridge in preparation for an attack. At their approach, the defenders threw down so many stones, spears and arrows that most ships were badly damaged. Olaf had had the idea of using wood from nearby houses to construct rafts and cover them with thatched roofs that could withstand anything thrown down. That way his troops safely rowed to the bridge and attached cables around its supportive piles. They then rowed away until the structure loosened, cracked and fell into the Thames. Some of the Danish soldiers fled to the Southwark defence where they were attacked and defeated. Others in the castle, seeing this and the bridge's collapse, surrendered and Ethelred assumed his crown again

Olaf returned to Norway and died in battle in 1030. He was canonized the following year.

How Great was Alfred?

When King Alfred of the Saxons captured London in 886AD, he was already one of England's greatest heroes. Born in 849AD, he had ruled the kingdom of Wessex south of the Thames since 871AD and that year fought nine battles against the Vikings to save it. He was forced to retreat in 878AD to a fort in the marshes of Athelney in Somerset, but harassed the Vikings from there and secretly built up an army that surprised and defeated a larger Viking army in Edington, Wiltshire. He also created the first English navy for which he would design large ships to command the sea.

Alfred launched his offensive campaign against London in 886AD and defeated a Viking garrison. Londoners gave him their enthusiastic support, as did other English people not ruled by the Danish Vikings. London was then part of the kingdom of Mercia, and Alfred turned control of the city over to Ethelred, a Mercian and his future son-in-law. Alfred fortified the old Roman walls and gave residents plots of land if they would help defend the city. These plots shaped the street plan that still exists between Cheapside and the Thames. In 893AD, Viking ships sailed up the river with a large army that encamped north of the city and attacked nearby towns and villages. When Alfred had the river blocked to imprison the ships, the army withdrew without marching on London.

Among the many accomplishments of his reign, Alfred founded 25 towns and two religious houses, rebuilt the monasteries the Vikings had destroyed, established and funded schools, published and enforced fair laws, ordered scholars to write the first history book, the *Anglo-Saxon Chronicle*, translated Latin books into the Anglo-Saxon language and even invented a candle clock.

Alfred died in 899AD having made Wessex a virtual fortress with a series of garrisoned forts that the Vikings could not overcome. His son, Edward, and Edward's son, Athelstan, expanded the kingdom to virtually the size of modern England.

London's Peace Guild

King Athelstan, who ruled from 925 to 939AD, introduced codes of law that had strict punishments for theft and corruption, but were lenient towards youthful offenders. Athelstan raised the age at which someone could be executed from 12 to 16. He also apologized in one of his law codes for the amount of crime during his reign: 'I am sorry my peace is kept so badly. My advisors say I have put up with it too long.'

BELOW: This heroic bronze statue of King Alfred the Great was erected in 1899 in Winchester where he died and was buried, having chosen the city as his capital. It stands next to the site of the city's East Gate.

ABOVE: King Athelstan died
in Gloucester and wished to
be buried in Malmesbury
Abbey. His remains were
lost during the Dissolution
of the Monasteries in
the Reformation, so his
fifteenth century tomb in
the abbey is empty.

Athelstan determined that a new policing method was needed for his lawless city. The new peace guild included nobles and clergy, London commoners and landowners in the surrounding counties. A series of rules and regulations were drawn up, and members pledged to support the King and his officials in keeping the peace. The 100 members were divided into groups of 10 with a leader, and each member pledged a shilling to pursue criminals. They held monthly meetings and reported their actions to the King. Guild members took an oath that included policing as well as social and spiritual obligations. Each paid four pence for social reasons. If a member died, each contributed a loaf and arranged for 50 psalms to be sung by himself or by paying someone to do it for him.

The St Brice's Day Massacre

King Ethelred II 'the Unready' had seen Danes attack his kingdom for several years, when he was warned in 1002 that the raiders would 'faithlessly take his life,' and that of all his councillors before ruling his kingdom. This led to his decree to kill 'all the Danish men who were among the English race.' This so-called St Brice's Day Massacre occurred on 13 November 1002, the saint's feast day. Danes found in London were murdered, as well as those in Bristol, Gloucester, Oxford and other areas. Ethelred later wrote that his decree had ordered that 'all the Danes who had sprung up in this island, sprouting like cockle [weeds] amongst the wheat, were to be destroyed by a most just extermination.'

'This led to his decree to kill all the Danish men who were among the English race.'

However, it was impossible to wipe out the large number of Danes living for years in the regions of the Danelaw in northern and eastern England. Neither did it stop the savage attacks by Viking warriors. One of the massacre's victims was the sister of Sweyn Forkbeard who retaliated in 1013: he attacked London, drove Ethelred to Normandy and became King himself.

In 2008, excavations at St John's College in Oxford uncovered 34 to 38 male skeletons aged between 16 and 35 who were victims of the massacre. The skulls of 27 were broken or cracked. One had been decapitated and five more suffered attempted decapitations, all from the front as they faced their executioners.

How Unready was Ethelred?

The King was actually known as 'Unraed,' meaning the ill-advised. Ethelred was a weak King who tried to buy off the raiding Vikings, paying 11,800kg (26,000lb) of silver between 991 to 994AD, but they still attacked his Anglo-Saxon subjects. He tried unsuccessfully again in 1002 with 10,900kg (24,000lb) of silver. Even his call for the St Brice's Day massacre backfired by causing Sweyn Forkbeard to take his crown. William Malmesbury, a twelfth-century historian, wrote that Ethelred's life was 'cruel in the beginning, wretched in the middle and disgraceful in the end.'

Edmund Ironsides

Edmund became King in the violent year of 1016. His father, King Ethelred II 'the Unready,' died that April, and Edmund was immediately faced with a siege of London by Knut Sveinsson (Canute), who had been named King, but not crowned by the witan (council) in Southampton. Edmund raised an army in Wessex and returned to break the siege. When he left again to find more troops, Canute resumed the siege, but Edmund once again ended it. His strong defence saved the city, and Londoners proclaimed him the new King, crowning him Edmund II in St Paul's Cathedral in April.

In subsequent battles against the Danish, Edmund fought so well he was given the nickname of 'Ironsides.' He defeated the enemy in Kent, but his forces were routed by Canute's men in Essex. Another battle loomed in Gloucestershire where Edmund supposedly tried to persuade Canute to fight him alone to save lives.

BELOW: After several battles that gave no final victory, King Edmund and Canute met on the island of Olney in the River Severn in Gloucestershire. Here they negotiated the peace treaty that divided England between them.

CANUTE AND THE TIDE

After Canute's death in 1035, stories spread throughout Britain and Europe about his remarkable triumphs, but one told of a situation Canute the Great could not conquer. According to Henry, Archdeacon of Huntingdon and twelfth-century chronicler, the King of England was carried down to the shore and told the tide it was subject to him, then ordered it to become still and stop breaking on his land and wetting his clothing. When the waves refused this demand, the devout Canute proclaimed, 'Let all the world know that the power of Kings is empty and worthless, and there is no King worthy of the name save Him by whose will heaven and earth and sea obey eternal laws.' After this, the Archdeacon added, Canute placed his golden crown on an image of Christ and never wore it again.

LEFT: The legend of Canute and the tide was a good way of showing his piety and the greater power of God.

Canute refused, citing Edmund's superior strength. Instead, they drew up a peace agreement that gave London, Wessex, Essex and East Anglia to Edmund and Mercia and Northumbria to Canute. It also proclaimed that whoever survived the longest would rule all this land.

Edmund died in suspicious circumstances a month later in December, after having ruled for only seven months. Canute then became 'King of all England.' With Edmund out of the way, Canute began a ruthless revenge, killing prominent Englishmen, including Edmund's brother, Eadwig, and turning their lands over to his own Danish supporters.

Two Sons of Canute

When Canute died, his illegitimate son, Harold Harefoot (named for his speed and hunting skills), became regent because his younger half-brother, Hardicanute – the legitimate heir to the throne – was away serving as King of Denmark. In 1036, Harold's men caught and blinded the claimant Alfred the Aetheling, who died of his wounds, and the next year Harold was crowned as Harold I. He also banished Hardicanute's mother, Queen Emma, the wife of Canute. Harold had a brief rule, dying in March 1040, as his brother was preparing to invade and claim his sovereignty. Hardicanute, along with his mother, arrived with 62 warships in June, marched to London and was crowned Canute II. He had his brother's remains removed from the abbey at Westminster, beheaded and tossed into a fen by the Thames. Others rescued the body and buried it in nearby St Clement Danes church.

Canute II was quickly unpopular, levelling a 'fleet-tax' on his subjects to pay for his invasion that was not needed. In June 1042, two years after assuming the throne, he had a seizure and collapsed with convulsions while drinking at a wild wedding feast. The crown then passed to Canute's stepson, Edward the Confessor.

Godwine, the Power behind the Throne

Even though he was an Anglo-Saxon, Godwine (also spelled Godwin) advanced to become close to Canute, who in 1018 named him the Earl of Essex. When Canute died in 1035, Godwine apparently made it possible for Edward the Confessor to become King after Canute's sons by being involved in the murder of the claimant Alfred the Aetheling. Godwine thus was able to control Edward and increased his own power as the real ruler of England for 11 years, even marrying his daughter Edith to the King.

'Canute began a ruthless revenge, killing prominent Englishmen.'

The two leaders fell out, however, over Edward's desire to bring more Normans into his court. When a Norman lord in Dover was opposed by his subjects in 1051, Godwine refused to punish them and the King exiled him. This did not last long, as Godwine and his son, Harold, invaded the next year. The nobles insisted that civil war be avoided, so Edward was forced to restore privileges and property to Godwine and his family. Many members of the King's Norman retinue were also exiled. When Godwine died in 1053, his son inherited the earldom and in 1066 succeeded the King, being crowned in London as Harold II.

William the Conqueror

When the Duke of Normandy and his French mistress had a son in 1028, the boy was taunted by locals as 'William the Bastard.' When his father died on a crusade, William became the duke and immediately faced rivals who plunged Normandy into conflict. With the help of the French King, he defeated his enemies and gave indications of his ruthless cruelty, cutting off the hands and feet of the prisoners.

BELOW: The Battle of Hastings was fought on Senlac Hill where Harold found his 5000 weary men facing William's 15,000. The English relied on a shield wall for their hopeless defence against the Norman archers and cavalry.

William's cousin, Edward, who would become Edward the Confessor, apparently promised William he could be his successor. Edward on his deathbed, however, named Harold, the earl who in 1063 had subjugated the Welsh, for the King. His coronation took place the day the King died in 1066. This infuriated William because he had rescued Harold from a French prison and received his promise to support William's claim to the throne.

By then, William's claim was finding support in France and even from the Pope. He was able to gather together an impressive force and some 700 ships for an invasion of the Sussex coast while Harold was in the north fighting Vikings. The King quickly marched against the invader and met William's force near Hastings in October 1066 in a battle where thousands were slaughtered and Harold was killed by an arrow through his eye.

> **'The new King waged one of the most brutal suppressions the country had ever known.'**

William next moved on London and encountered no resistance until the south end of London Bridge. He withdrew for a wide but speedy circling movement around the city, marching through three counties, burning and laying waste as he went. This created fear that brought Edgar the Aetheling, heir to the throne, and London leaders to meet William at Berkhamsted, Hertfordshire, to swear allegiance to the conqueror.

William was crowned on Christmas Day in Westminster Abbey, and immediately granted London a charter that allowed citizens to keep King Edward's laws and assured every child would be heir to his father, married or not. There were, however, more battles to come, and William began building a series of towers, including the Tower of London. The North continued to resist, and the new King waged one of the most brutal suppressions the country had ever known. He destroyed villages and farmlands, creating a dreadful famine, and deaths were estimated at about 100,000. By 1075, he had crushed all opposition and Norman efficiency took over the country. The most notable example was the Doomsday Book in which were recorded all of England's land holdings along with each farm animal.

William returned to France and was fatally injured at the Battle of Mantes in July 1087, when his horse reared and the saddle ruptured his intestines. He died five weeks later at the age of 59.

The Tower of London

As soon as he was crowned, William began to erect the tower that would become feared as a political prison and place of torture and execution. Situated on the north bank of the Thames, which once fed its moat, the Tower also guarded the city's port and served as an arsenal. The White Tower in the centre was constructed around 1078 of limestone that came aptly from Normandy. Future additions around it have included 13 towers, one named the Bloody Tower. By the thirteenth century, a watergate was used as the entrance for prisoners being brought by the river, and was nicknamed 'Traitors' Gate.'

Those executed within its walls included Sir Thomas More, Henry VIII's wives Anne Boleyn and Catherine Howard, Lady Jane Grey, Thomas Cromwell and probably the adolescent King Edward V and his younger brother. Among others imprisoned there were James I of Scotland, Henry VI, the future Elizabeth I, Sir Walter Raleigh, Guy Fawkes and Samuel Pepys.

OPPOSITE: The Tower of London is visited by some 3 million tourists a year. Highlights include the Crown Jewels, the Beefeaters (officially 'yeoman warders') and the ravens, which, legend says, would cause the kingdom to fall if they leave.

THE MEDIEVAL CITY

A growing London meant the beginning of larger conflicts among powers determined to rule the city and nation. Its dark streets were riddled with crime, but the Crown provided the worst persecutions, tortures and murders.

LONDON HAD BECOME England's largest town by the eleventh century, serving as the centre for the Crown and Church. When William the Conqueror and his Norman army defeated and killed King Harold at the Battle of Hastings in 1066, Londoners were confident they could resist with reinforcements. William moved swiftly, however, to isolate the city and it quickly surrendered. The residents, in fact, became staunch supporters of their new King, who issued a charter granting them large measures of freedom and also justice.

Despite this hopeful beginning, medieval London was dark and dangerous. Rulers used its Tower to torture and execute all types of dissidents and possible claimants to the throne. Neither did they spare the powerful Church, as when Henry II had his Archbishop of Canterbury Thomas Becket murdered in 1170. Common Londoners also viewed death during the public hangings, which were used to both warn and entertain the crowds. The worst offenders faced the grisly

OPPOSITE: The murder of Archbishop Thomas Becket was especially shocking because it was committed in his cathedral. The four knights brutally attacked him at twilight in the north transept near the altar of the Virgin Mary.

ABOVE: William the Conqueror and his army rode through the streets of London in triumph after the success of his Norman invasion. As William I, he brought strong leadership (and the French language) to the English throne.

OPPOSITE: Matilda's escape from Oxford Castle was made in the dead of night. Wearing white as a disguise, she walked through the snow to Abingdon. People still claim to see her ghost in a white cape in the castle.

penalty of being drawn – dragged through the streets to the place of execution on a wooden frame by horses – and quartered. Even minor crimes brought severe penalties: a robber could have a hand amputated or sometimes a foot.

The Anarchy

An early civil war in England was fought between the daughter and nephew of Henry I and was popularly known as the Anarchy.

Since his son had died, Henry nominated his daughter, Matilda, also called Maud, as his successor, but Stephen of Blois claimed his uncle had changed his mind on his deathbed and chose him. The Church and powerful barons supported his claim, unhappy to be ruled by a woman and one who was arrogant and married to their enemy, Geoffrey Plantagenet, Count of Anjou. At Henry's death in 1135, Stephen was given the crown and battled throughout his 19-year reign to keep it. During this period, supporters on each side terrorized the countryside, destroying crops and stealing cattle, sheep and supplies. It was an era, a chronicler noted, when 'Christ and his saints slept.'

Matilda and her half-brother, Robert of Gloucester, landed in 1139, and the war's first big battle was two years later in Lincoln. Stephen's force was defeated and Matilda had him imprisoned in Bristol Castle for a while. He was released in exchange for Robert, and soon Matilda was captured and held in Devizes Castle in Wiltshire. In 1141, she escaped disguised as a corpse tied on a funeral bier and was carried in that manner to Gloucester. She went to London the same year, but was never crowned, forced to leave by the population who disliked her haughtiness – she used the title of Empress – and her audacity of asking for money. The next year, she was captured once more and imprisoned in Oxford Castle, again escaping while dressed in white to blend in with the freezing snow and then crossing the frozen Thames there.

Robert died in 1147 and Matilda retired to Normandy for the remainder of her life. Her son, Henry of Anjou, then invaded and was soundly defeated by Stephen's army. In 1153, after his son died, Stephen agreed with Henry to the Treaty of Wallingford making Stephen King for life and then having Henry crowned. Stephen lived for less than a year, and Henry II became the first Plantagenet King in 1154, reigning for 35 years. Matilda died in 1167.

A Dreadful Way to Die

Execution by drawing and quartering for treason was ordained in England in 1287, but had existed at least 50 years earlier. This public torture began with the prisoner being tied to a horse and dragged (drawn) to the gallows. Since this in itself might kill the condemned, he was sometimes placed on a wooden hurdle or frame for the trip. He was then hanged, but cut down while still alive to be castrated, disembowelled and to watch his genitalia and entrails burned. The final terror involved beheading and cutting his body into quarters. Sometimes horses were used for quartering, tying the prisoner's four limbs to four horses and driving them in different directions to accomplish the gruesome division.

The first renowned traitor to suffer such an execution was the Welsh prince, David ap Gruffydd, who rebelled against the English occupation of his country until captured in 1283. He was drawn and quartered that year in Shrewsbury for plotting King Edward I's death.

London's most famous prisoner was Scotland's great hero Sir William Wallace who also fought against English rule. He was apprehended in 1305 and marched to London to be paraded through the city. He disputed the charge of treason, arguing that he had never sworn allegiance to King Edward I and was therefore not a traitor. Nevertheless, his execution took place the same year, with Wallace forced to wear a crown of laurel leaves as he was whipped and pelted with waste on the way to the gallows in Smithfield. He was drawn for treason, hanged for robbery and homicide, disembowelled for sacrilege, beheaded for being an outlaw and finally quartered for 'divers depredations.' For good measure his heart was also removed from his chest. Lastly, Wallace's head was placed on London Bridge and his quarters sent to four other cities.

Murder and Mayhem

Murder was a constant threat on London's filthy twisted streets and alleyways, often from vicious gangs. On 16 June 1298, a group of 16 armed robbers attacked paupers near St Paul's Cathedral, causing the deaths of 144, some cut down and others trampled in the panic to flee. Riots were also part of the city's disorderly growth. Its craft guilds grew in power and number, with at least 50 existing in 1377 and 111 by 1400. Their competition to regulate trade, prices and wages led to pitched street battles. As early as 1267, the Goldsmiths and Taylors fought a bloody engagement that killed many of the 500 fighters and led to the execution of their leaders.

London was even the target of rebellions that began in the countryside, particularly the Peasants' Revolt of 1381 and Cade's Rebellion in 1450. Religious heresy was particularly feared and led to persecutions, such as the one befalling the Lollards in the fifteenth century that saw one of their leaders, William Sawtre, burned at the stake in London.

OPPOSITE: William Wallace was strapped to a wooden hurdle to be dragged to the execution site. After his death, quarters of his body were sent to Newcastle-on-Tyne and the Scottish towns of Berwick, Stirling and Perth.

'The final terror involved beheading and cutting his body into quarters.'

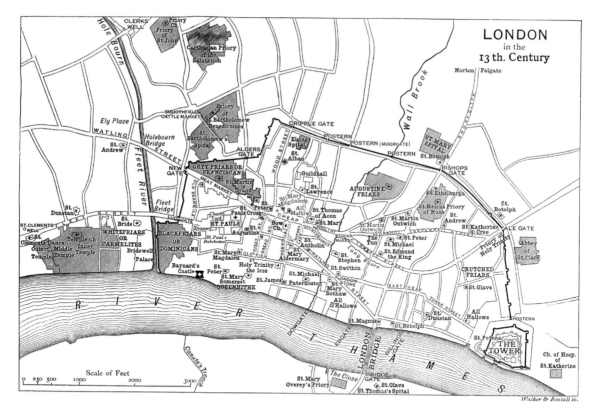

LONDON
in the
13th. Century

Walker & Boutall sc.

ABOVE: **By the beginning of the thirteenth century, London's population had grown to nearly 30,000. The city limits had hardly expanded, and residents lived in crowded and cramped neighbourhoods. Few developments existed across the river and Westminster was a separate village.**

Nightwalkers

London's medieval streets were especially dangerous, and residents feared to go out after dark and encounter 'nightwalkers,' a general term for those loitering with criminal intent, such as young toughs and thieves. Some of the most dangerous would blacken their faces. Not as dangerous, but equally to be avoided, were drunks, vagrants, beggars, seducers and prostitutes. Edward I ordered watches on the streets from sundown to sunup, saying 'if any Stranger do pass by them' the nightwalkers should be held until morning and taken to the sheriff. In fact, gentlemen out at night were seldom questioned, but anyone from the lower classes risked arrest. In 1282, the Mayor of London opened a prison in Cornhill for 'night-walkers and other suspicious persons.' It was named the Tun because the shape resembled a large tun of ale. In 1331, Edward III issued a statute defining nightwalkers as 'such persons as sleep by day and walk by night, being oftentimes pilferers, or disturbers of the peace.'

Trial by Ordeal

Before Pope Innocent III disallowed the practice in 1215, the guilt or innocence of suspects was often decided in the presence of priests by primitive trials based on magic and superstition. Outcomes in London and throughout the country could be decided by barbaric tests variously involving fire, water, combat and even the indications of a corpse.

Those given an ordeal by fire had to carry a red-hot bar of iron for three paces. If his hand showed no burns, he was judged innocent; if burns were suffered, the verdict was guilty and he was quickly hanged. In some cases, his burned hand was bandaged to see if it healed in three days to prove innocence. Ethelred the

Unready decreed that 'untrustworthy men' must hold an iron three times as heavy. A variation involved plunging the right hand into boiling water to pull out a ring. Another fire ordeal was to have the suspect run over nine ploughshares that were heated white-hot. Perhaps worse was the ordeal of licking a red-hot iron.

A slightly less painful test involved binding up suspects and tossing them into water that had been blessed, on the theory that God would save the innocent. The verdict was innocent if they sank and guilty if they floated, with the defendant fished out to be hanged. This was often a preferred ordeal because of the instant result.

An ordeal by combat, introduced by the Normans, was normally reserved for nobles. It gave an accuser the right to fight the person who might have wronged him. If a land dispute was involved, both could choose another to fight for him, and these often turned out to be professionals. In some instances, the defendant had the right to choose to battle his accuser.

BELOW: Trial by water was based on an old test for witches. Since a witch had supposedly refused to be baptized, the theory said water would reject her body and she would float. Sinking meant innocence but perhaps death.

More strange was the idea that a corpse could show who was guilty. The torment in this case was mental. The trial by bier had suspects brought before the body in the presence of the coroner. If the dried wounds of the victim began to bleed again, guilt was established.

The priests in charge of obtaining proof sometimes fixed the outcome, since they believed only the innocent would agree to such torture. With this in mind, they could make sure the water was not actually boiling or the iron burning hot. When trials by ordeals were banned, jury trials by peers replaced them. Defendants at first refused this justice, since they mistrusted their peers, believing many wished to use a guilty verdict for revenge or jealousy. Those who baulked at jury trials were in some cases tortured to bring them to court.

Murder in the Cathedral

Thomas Becket was born about 1120 in London's Cheapside, the son of a Norman merchant. He studied Canon law in France and in 1154 was named Archdeacon of Canterbury.

Thomas Becket surprised King Henry by becoming a strong Archbishop. The King had appointed him as a close friend and supporter, but Becket became a devout and authoritarian church leader who lectured the King and his knights.

That year King Henry II appointed him as Lord Chancellor handling the King's revenue. He became the trusted advisor and close friend of Henry who was some 15 years younger. In 1162, a Royal commission elected him Archbishop of Canterbury. Henry expected him to be a docile head of the Church, but Becket began to expand the powers of his office and refused to sign documents reducing his independence. He was charged with contempt of Royal authority and in 1164 escaped to France for six years until Henry compromised and reinstated him.

Now back in Canterbury, Becket began to excommunicate priests who had opposed him, including the Bishop of London. On Christmas Day 1170, Becket again excommunicated more enemies. When word of this reached the King at his Christmas court in Normandy, he railed against his own shameful treatment by this 'low-born cleric' and accused his knights of the household of letting it happen. His words were later quoted as 'Who will rid me of this troublesome priest?' Given this anger and perhaps misinterpreting Henry's words, four knights crossed the English Channel to Canterbury on 29 December 1170 to confront Becket. When he refused their demand to submit to Henry's will and restore those

'Another assassin cut away the top of Becket's head with one stroke.'

he had excommunicated, each knight attacked with a sword. Becket stood after a blow to his head, but fell to his knees and elbows after another strike. 'For the name of Jesus and the protection of the Church,' he said, 'I am ready to embrace death.' Another assassin cut away the top of Becket's head with one stroke, and his brains and blood spilled onto the floor. Then a clerk who had accompanied the knights pressed his foot against the dead man's neck and scattered more blood and gore about, shouting, 'Let us away, knights. This fellow will arise no more.' The assassins were soon excommunicated by Pope Alexander III who ordered them to serve in the Holy Lands for 14 years.

Pope Alexander III made Becket a saint in 1173 and pilgrims flocked to see the grave of the martyr in Canterbury Cathedral, as Chaucer wrote in *Canterbury Tales*. Londoners, who had preferred to call him Thomas of London, made their native a patron saint with St Paul. In 1174, Henry made a public penance at his tomb. In 1538, King Henry VIII ordered Becket's shrine and bones to be destroyed during his dissolution of the monasteries.

Massacre of the Jews

Richard I was the son of the Plantagenet King Henry II and would gain fame as Richard the Lionheart on the Third Crusade to the Holy Land, during which he was imprisoned by Leopold, the Duke of Austria, until a ransom of 150,000 gold marks was paid. During his 10-year reign of crusades, he spent less than a year in England, only using it to finance his adventures. 'I would have sold London itself,' he supposedly declared, 'if I could have found a rich enough buyer.'

Richard's coronation on 3 September 1189 was in some way an indication of the blood that would be spilled in coming years over religious convictions. He issued an edict banning Jews from his coronation, but some of them brought presents for him and approached where he was dining. Local people threw insults and chased after them, telling others that the King had called for the massacre of all Jews. Londoners began killing those at hand and broke into Jewish houses to murder the residents and plunder their property. Some victims barricaded themselves inside, but the mob set the houses on fire and killed them.

OPPOSITE: To kill Becket, the assassins had to invade the monastic cloister and chapel where he was assisting with vespers. They ordered him to leave the cathedral, but Becket refused, forcing them to commit murder right before the altar.

Others were allowed or forced to become baptized Christians. Richard, who received financial backing from Jews, ordered their protection after being told of the massacre. He also demanded the names of those responsible. The worst murderers were executed, but many rioters had otherwise good reputations and were not prosecuted.

Other cities imitated the London massacre, including Norwich, Lincoln and York. In the latter, some 150 Jews retreated to the castle where they were besieged. Fearing they could not defend it, men killed their wives and children, throwing their dead bodies from the walls onto people below before committing suicide. When the castle was taken, the surviving Jews were murdered. Others burned their own houses and died inside. Many people who owed money to the Jews went to the cathedral where their records of debts were kept and burned them.

Executed by Poker?

Edward II was a feeble, unintelligent and bumbling King, reigning from 1307 to 1327. One of his favourite interests was digging ditches. He struggled to reduce the power of barons and frequently had opponents hanged or beheaded. His biggest troubles lay in Scotland, where Robert I, popularly known as Robert the Bruce, was extending his power. Edward led his army north and suffered a devastating defeat at the Battle of Bannockburn on 24 June 1314 that assured Scotland's independence. He did have success finally against a major English rival, Thomas of Lancaster, who by 1314 virtually controlled the country through the parliament of York. Edward defeated him on 16 March 1322 at the Battle of Boroughbridge and had him executed six days later.

The King made a fatal move by supporting Hugh le Despenser and his son. They made administrative reforms that made them wealthy and created an enemy of Queen Isabella, Edward's wife, whose lands were seized in 1324. After residing in France for 18 months, along with their son, the future Edward III, Queen Isabella and her lover, Sir Roger Mortimer, returned with an army that captured the King and the Despensers as they fled west. The latter were executed and Edward imprisoned at Kenilworth Castle in Warwickshire. A revolutionary parliament declared him incompetent to govern and chose Edward III as King. Edward II abdicated and was taken to Berkeley Castle, Gloucestershire, in April 1327. Here he underwent torture that included starvation and being thrown into a pit of rotting corpses. After the failure of two rescues, he was executed in September.

Legend has it that Edward was killed at night by a group of assassins who inserted a horn into his rectum and through that pushed a red-hot poker that burned away his organs. This was reported by the contemporary historian Geoffrey le Baker, but some suspected the account was propaganda from those favouring the deposed King.

OPPOSITE: Slaughter swept the streets as the massacre of Jews intensified. The mindless violence grew so out of hand that even Christian homes and families were attacked. Despite the many atrocities, no official was ever blamed.

BELOW: Edward II, shown here with his jailers, suffered a physical collapse after the intense tortures he underwent. He knew all was lost after the executions of the Dispensers and the deaths of three of his four sons.

Tyburn's First Noble Victim

Roger Mortimer was the cousin of Edward II and Edward's Queen Isabella, who was his mistress and plotted with him to murder her husband in 1327. Mortimer then ruled as regent for three years before the young Edward III could take the throne.

'Mortimer became the first of his class to be hanged at Tyburn.'

Mortimer had an impressive military life, fighting in 1308 in Ireland and in 1314 at the Battle of Bannockburn in Scotland. In 1321, he had opposed the King's favourites, the Despensers (father and son) and the following year was imprisoned in the Tower. He escaped in 1323 to France and was joined after two years by Isabella, who became his lover. They invaded England in 1326 and overthrew Edward II and the Despensers, then arranged the King's murder. During his regency, Mortimer accumulated wealth and titles, making enemies of his peers. Henry of Lancaster convinced 17-year-old Edward III that Mortimer had a plot to seize the throne. The King had him arrested on 19 October 1330 in Nottingham Castle and imprisoned in the Tower of London. He was tried in parliament bound in chains and ropes and wearing a gag to prevent him from speaking as he was charged with the murder of Edward II and his half-brother, the Earl of Kent. The verdict was a resounding 'Guilty'.

BELOW: Roger Mortimer's downfall came when Edward III's men surprised and arrested him in Nottingham Castle. His remaining supporters drifted away, because his arrogance and greed had alienated fellow barons and peers in Parliament.

On 29 November 1330, Mortimer was taken to Tyburn to be executed. He was forced to wear the black tunic he had worn for Edward II's funeral and was dragged behind two horses. His clothes were stripped from him, and he made a short speech, admitting to his role in Kent's death, but nothing more. Noblemen were normally beheaded, with hanging reserved for common criminals, so Mortimer became the first of his class to be hanged at Tyburn.

The Peasants' Revolt

Considered the first great people's rebellion, the Peasants' Revolt in 1381 began as an uprising against a new poll tax that was three times as much as the previous year. Also called Wat Tyler's Rebellion after its leader, the revolt resisted tax collectors, sought to end feudal serfdom and protested several economic grievances, such as the Crown's attempt to cap wages following a labour shortage after the Black Death. The protest began in May in Essex and spread across the southeast. In June, the Essex men were joined by a force from Kent led by Tyler. He marched them into London on the 13th where they massacred Flemish merchants, set fire to a treasury building and destroyed the palace of the Duke of Lancaster, uncle of King Richard II. This was enough to compel Richard to meet with the Essex peasants the next day outside the city to receive their petition and to promise reforms.

ABOVE: As the peasants approached London, King Richard II went from Windsor to the Tower of London for his protection. Other defences were not in place by the time the rebels began street attacks, joined by some poor Londoners.

ABOVE: King Richard II and his soldiers met the rebelling peasants outside the city walls. Most of the rebels still respected their King and obeyed his order to return home, believing his false guarantee of pardons.

While this happened, Tyler's men captured the Tower of London and beheaded the two men they blamed for the poll tax, the government's treasurer and chancellor, along with the uncle's physician. Richard and his retinue met Tyler and his force the next day at Smithfields, where the King again promised to make reforms. When Tyler addressed him in a rude manner, the London mayor jerked him from his horse and a squire fatally struck him. Richard instantly stood up to the angry peasants, promising the reforms they sought and urging them to follow him back through the city. The trip was soon ended, however, when the mayor's troops surrounded the rebels. Richard gave them pardons and convinced them to return home.

The worst of the month-long rebellion was crushed, but riots continued in other towns, such as Cambridge where peasants and sympathetic locals damaged some of the university and burned its archives. Although the future poll tax was halted, the King denied he had agreed to any of the peasants' demands and revoked his pardons. Those leaders still at large were found and executed.

> 'Crowds arrived early to get a spot close to the scaffold and sit in the open galleries.'

A Fine Day for a Hanging

Medieval London was nicknamed 'the City of Gallows' for its many locations for hangings, such as Tyburn, Tower Hill and Smithfield. These gruesome executions drew hundreds of spectators, even thousands for renowned prisoners, and the atmosphere had the bustle and liveliness of a festival or carnival. Samuel Johnson said of hangings, 'If they don't draw spectators, they don't answer their purpose.' Crowds arrived early to get a spot close to the scaffold and sit in the open galleries erected for the best view, while others perched on roofs or sat comfortably at windows or on balconies, often for a fee. Many viewers were women, noble and otherwise. Booths and carts were positioned among the crowd to sell food, drink and souvenirs. The entertainment (other than the execution itself) included jugglers, dancers and minstrels.

Many had come for a fun and exciting day out, so their behaviour often was irreverent and boisterous as they enjoyed 'collar day.' They heckled the condemned as he gave his last speech, laughed at those who lost their nerve and struggled, yelled to the hangman to 'get on with it' and particularly enjoyed seeing family and friends pull on the legs of a victim swinging on the rope to assure he had a quick death and not suffer. The crowd's insults could also turn on authorities when the condemned was a popular or presumed innocent figure, giving him cheers, applause and encouragement.

BELOW: Those who regularly attended hangings were given a special treat when several victims were executed together. More mementoes were available, such as the hangman's ropes that were cut into pieces and sold as morbid souvenirs.

Fights broke out among spectators, especially drunk ones. People would rush to touch the body and clip its hair, because this supposedly offered cures for diseases. Since the executioner was given the clothes of his victim, family members had to buy them back if they wished, and this created angry haggling. Friends of the dead often battled with those who came for unclaimed bodies that had been sold to surgeons for dissection.

'He was hanged and burned after he had asked God to forgive his enemies.'

Lollards at the Stake

John Sawtre was a Roman Catholic priest in Norfolk who followed the teachings of John Wycliffe, founder of the Lollard movement. Among the changes this reformation advocated was access to the Bible for everyone, marriage for priests, condemnation of the Church's wealth and the rejection of the Pope, transubstantiation at the mass, saints and confessions. For his beliefs, Sawtre was arrested in 1399 and denounced Lollardy, promising not to preach the doctrine. In 1401, however, he moved to a London church and again advocated Lollard tenets. He was summoned to St Paul's Cathedral where Archbishop Thomas Arundel charged him with heresy. Sawtre was bold enough to express disbelief in the Eucharist, saying 'it remained very bread and the same bread which was before the words were spoken.' He was convicted and sentenced to death with the decree that he 'should be degraded in public in detestation of such crime, and in manifest example of other Christians.' Sawtre was taken in March to Smithfield to be the first Lollard burned at the stake, a few days before parliament passed a statute making this the punishment for heresy. John Purvey, a Lollard friend of Sawtre, was among several other priests burned for heresy.

BELOW: Lollards were paraded through the streets and put through other public humiliations before being burned at the stake. The movement went underground to survive and was able to play a role during the English Reformation.

Sir John Oldcastle, a distinguished warrior knight, suffered the same fate in 1417 and became a Lollard hero. A former friend of Henry V before he became King, Oldcastle was charged in March 1413 for supporting Lollard preachers and opinions. The Archbishop of Canterbury called him 'the principal harbourer, promoter, protector and defender of heretics.' Oldcastle also had to face Archbishop Arundel and was imprisoned in the Tower of London. He escaped in October and retreated to his castle to organize a large group of Lollards throughout the country to march on London. They were met in St Giles's Fields by the King's forces who quickly routed them. Oldcastle went into hiding, but was captured in late 1417. He appeared before parliament before being taken to the Tower where he was hanged and burned after he had asked God to forgive his enemies.

Lollardy was forced underground, but resurfaced about 1500 and suffered more martyrs. Within three decades it merged with new Protestant movements.

ABOVE: Sir John Oldcastle suffered the unusual execution of being hanged over fire that then burned the gallows. He was taken from the Tower to St Giles's Fields, so he would die at the scene of his revolt.

A Duke's House of Witches

Eleanor, Duchess of Gloucester, had often used the potions and spells of Margery Jourdemayne, well known in London as the 'Witch of Eye.' This magic, it was said, allowed Eleanor to captivate and marry Humphrey, the Duke of Gloucester. He was a heartbeat away from the throne, being the uncle of Henry VI and having served as regent before Henry assumed the crown at the age of 16.

Henry's death would therefore benefit the ambitious Eleanor, and she turned again to Margery. The Witch of Eye made her several wax dolls wearing crowns and these figures were thrown into the fire each day to melt away. Unfortunately, three of the scholars of the duke's court, servants to Eleanor, were involved and word got out. They then implicated the duchess and she in turn implicated Margery. In 1441, all five were rounded

up on the charge of treasonable witchcraft, using black magic to cause the death of the King.

The duchess was found guilty of heresy and witchcraft, but not treason. Her marriage was annulled and she was forced to do penance walking around London. Her husband was proven to be unaware of the witchcraft. He retired and after three years was arrested on another treason charge, dying three days later in prison.

One of Eleanor's three courtiers, Roger Bolingbroke, an astrologer who communicated with the spirits of the dead, admitted his part and was hanged, drawn and quartered at Tyburn on 18 November 1441. Another died in prison, probably after taking poison, and the third who knew about the plot, but did not participate, received a Royal pardon.

Margery, the only one of humble birth, was a repeat offender, having been imprisoned for sorcery in 1432 at Windsor Castle and released when she promised not to practice again. She was therefore found guilty and on 27 October 1441 was burned at the stake in Smithfield.

Cade's Rebellion

Jack Cade, a former soldier, organized and led a rebellion of small landholders and some peasants in Kent in 1450. Among their numbers were a rector and prior. The rebels were infuriated by high taxes, forced labour and the seizure of their land. Although an Irishman, the charismatic Cade assumed the name of John Mortimer to identify with Richard, the Duke of York and the rival of King Henry VI.

A King's army sent to Kent to disperse the rebels was defeated at Sevenoaks by Cade's men. He then led them to storm London where he found some support from locals, until the city saw their violent behaviour. After nearly taking the Tower of London, they beheaded the Archbishop of Canterbury and the Lord High Treasurer, placing their heads on poles positioned as if they were kissing each other. They also executed the Sheriff of Kent. Local officials agreed to a truce and promised to meet Cade's list of demands. They also offered pardons to the attackers, including Cade. As the revolt died, however, the King ordered Cade's arrest and he fled the city. The new sheriff of Kent caught up with him in Sussex, and Cade was fatally wounded, dying on the return journey to London. His body was hanged, beheaded, drawn and quartered as if he was alive, and his head displayed on a pole on London Bridge. Although unsuccessful, Cade's rebellion was one of the key events that brought on the War of the Roses. Shakespeare dramatized the uprising in *Henry VI*.

OPPOSITE: The public penance of Eleanor involved holding a wax taper and walking from Temple Bar to St Paul's Cathedral where she offered it at the altar. She made two similar walks in other parts of the city.

BELOW: Among those executed by Jack Cade and his rebels was the Lord High Treasurer, James Fiennes, the 1st Baron Saye and Sele. They took him from the Tower, where he was imprisoned, and beheaded him in Cheapside.

THE RACK

The Tower of London was begun about 1078 by William the Conqueror as his fortress on the north bank of the Thames. He erected what is known as the White Tower and others, including the Bloody Tower, were added in the twelfth and thirteenth centuries. State prisoners in medieval days were transported down the river to 'Traitors' Gate' and would suffer extreme torture so that information and confessions could be extracted, or simply persecuted to wreak vengeance.

Ingenious devices were invented to inflict the most pain. Especially feared was the rack, introduced to the Tower about 1447 by the Duke of Exeter and nicknamed 'The Duke of Exeter's Daughter' and used by the Constable who had overall control of the Tower.

The instrument consisted of an open rectangular frame with rollers at both ends. Strong ropes were used to fasten a prisoner's wrists to one roller and his ankles to the other. The interrogator slowly turned an attached handle to stretch the victim's body. This would result in the dislocation of the victim's arms and legs, sometimes ripping off limbs. The rack was one of the slowest forms of torture and caused excruciating pain. A later medieval addition were spikes placed under the body to penetrate the spine and pull it apart. Prisoners 'broken on the rack' were often left with useless arms and legs, with many suffering paralysis or even death as a consequence.

RIGHT: The rack was seldom used, but some believe one victim was Guy Fawkes, who tried to blow up parliament.

The Murder of Royals

Dealing with English Kings was seldom easy, but London's growing commercial wealth and support of strong government gave it a special autonomy. Its citizens had elected a mayor since 1191, and rich merchants began to control their city, winning the approval of the sovereign who often sought their advice.

Behind the scenes, Royal intrigues and struggles continued. The death of King Henry VI in the Tower raised strong suspicions. From 1453 to 1455 Henry had suffered a mental breakdown or bout of insanity, which was inherited from his mother's family. The year he recovered, the 'mad king' was drawn into the War of the Roses between the houses of Lancaster and York who both claimed the throne. Henry's Queen, Margaret, was the driving force supporting the Lancastrian side. Shakespeare described her as possessing 'a tiger's heart wrapped in a woman's hide.' When their forces were defeated in 1461 in a snowstorm, the victor declared himself King Edward IV, and Henry fled to Scotland with his wife and son. He returned in 1464 and was captured the next year by Edward. The powerful Earl of Warwick restored Henry to the throne in 1470, but Warwick was killed on 14 April 1471 by Edward's army at the Battle of Barnet, north of London. Another victory by Edward at the Battle of Tewkesbury on 4 May killed Henry's only son and ended the War of the Roses with this Yorkist triumph. Henry was imprisoned in the Tower that year and stabbed to death on the night of 21 May, possibly by Edward IV's brother, Richard, the Duke of Gloucester, who later became Richard III. Henry's wife was also held in the Tower, but ransomed and lived out her life in her native Anjou, France.

After his death, the mild and pious King was venerated and a movement began to declare him a saint. He was credited with 174 miracles, which included restoring life to those killed by the plague, and pilgrims flocked to be healed at his grave in Chertsey Abbey, Surrey, and later in St George's Chapel at Windsor.

ABOVE: Henry VI became King at the age of nine months, and England was ruled for two decades by his uncles and cousins. Henry was a child when Joan of Arc led French forces against his troops.

LEFT: Richard Neville, the Earl of Warwick, was slain leading the Lancastrian army at the Battle of Barnet. 'The Kingmaker' fought on foot to show he would not leave his men and was killed while fleeing.

London Under Cannon Fire

The War of the Roses had been won, but the news came late to the illegitimate son of the Earl of Kent, Thomas Neville, nicknamed the 'Bastard of Fauconberg.' An expert sailor, Neville was given the Freedom of the City of London in 1454 for defeating pirates in the English Channel and North Sea. He fought on both sides during the war, first commanding part of Edward IV's Yorkist navy in 1470. The following year, he was appointed Vice Admiral of Lancaster's fleet by the Earl of Warwick and set his sights on taking London. On 8 May 1471, while King Edward's army was in the West Country, Neville wrote to London authorities saying he had a commission from Warwick and asked permission to peacefully march through the city to restore King Henry VI, who was imprisoned

THE LITTLE PRINCES

Richard III was one of England's most notorious Kings. His brother, King Edward IV, died in 1483 at the age of 21, and Richard became the guardian of Edward's sons, Edward, 12, and Richard, nine. Edward became an uncrowned King, but reigned for only two months. Richard declared their father's marriage invalid and their births illegitimate, and he had the two boys seized from their family and imprisoned in the Tower. They both disappeared that summer, surely murdered on their uncle's order. A history by Thomas More said the killers entered the princes' bedchamber and pushed the featherbed and pillows hard over their mouths until they were dead. One of Richard's servant knights, Sir James Tyrell, confessed to the murders under torture before being executed for treason in 1502. Shakespeare also named him in his play *Richard III*.

Richard had a short reign. On 22 August 1485, he was killed in Leicestershire during the last major battle of the War of the Roses by Henry of Richmond, who became King Henry VII.

In 1674, workers renovating the White Tower discovered the skeletons of two children under a staircase and 'heap of stones.' Four years later, they were buried in Westminster Abbey.

RIGHT: When the princes' bodies were never found, some believed they were alive. In 1491, a man in Ireland claimed to be the younger prince.

in the Tower. When the mayor and city corporation informed him that Warwick was dead and the Lancastrians defeated, Thomas expressed disbelief. Urged to recognize Edward as King, he refused and launched an attack.

On 12 May, a week after the Battle of Tewkesbury had ended Lancastrian hopes, the admiral sailed up the Thames and met his arriving army of some 20,000 Kentish and Essex men at Southwark. That day his force attacked London Bridge, burning down its new gate, but were eventually stopped by its defenders. Two days later he gathered 5000 rebels who pulled cannons from his ships and lined them along the south bank. They exchanged shots with the Tower's artillery, which proved more damaging and succeeded in pushing Neville's force back. He tried a three-pronged attack next, launching most of his men at London Bridge while sending some 3000 to take Aldgate and Bishopsgate. All three attacks failed. When the invaders broke into Aldgate, the defenders closed the gates and killed them all. A London force then made a counterattack and killed about 700 and took hundreds prisoner. On 18 May, the first of Edwards' army returned from Coventry. Thomas dismissed his men and handed over his 56 ships to the King who, accepting his loyalty, pardoned and knighted him, making him Vice Admiral of the Fleet.

> ## 'His head was returned to London to be displayed on the bridge.'

Four months later, the King's wrath proved stronger than his word. Thomas was arrested by the Duke of York in Southampton, taken to Yorkshire and beheaded in Middleham Castle. His head was returned to London to be displayed on the bridge he had tried to capture.

Fire and Plague

If man's inhumanity to man was not enough, ordinary Londoners faced major catastrophes that threatened their existence just as they were enjoying more material comforts. Three large fires occurred in 1087, 1136 and 1212 destroying many of the crowded houses made of wood with straw or thatched roofs. The Black Death made its first appearance in 1348 and severe outbreaks of the plague returned in 1361 and 1368. London and the rest of England with a population of nearly five million lost between one-third and one-half of a generation.

A major tragedy struck the city during the second week of July 1212, when fire raged south of the Thames. The Great Fire of Southwark, as it was called, totally consumed the cathedral church, St Mary Overie, and many buildings. High winds then swept the flames towards the old London Bridge where wooden houses and shops had been built on the stone foundations. Already the bridge was congested with people fleeing from Southwark who met rescuers coming from the opposite direction. By freak fate, cinders had blown over the bridge to land at its northern end, trapping the terrified crowd on the crossing. When the wooden buildings began to burn, many leaped into the river to drown or climb into rescue boats, some of which sank. The fire continued its path in the central city that had no organized fire brigade, and one account in 1603 estimated it killed more than 3000 people. This is thought to be overstated, but the fire still killed more than London's Great Fire of 1666.

The Black Death

The terrible plague arrived in Dorset in 1348 on a ship from France and swiftly reached London that year, causing the most deaths between February and May.

A RIVER OF REFUSE

The Thames determined the birthplace of London and its continued health. During the Middle Ages, however, the river's health was in serious doubt. Edward III described the river's 'fumes and other abominable stenches' in 1357 because 'dung and other filth had accumulated in divers places.' By then it had become a virtual sewer used to dump human waste, animal parts and blood from slaughterhouses and the runoff from many commercial and industrial businesses. The problem was greatly increased by 11 latrines built over tributaries to the Thames and two on London Bridge that emptied directly into the river below. Passing ships also dumped their waste into the water. Despite all this, many Londoners washed their clothes in the river, transferring the stench to what they wore.

The disease, known then as the Great Mortality, was a powerful combination of bubonic and pneumonic plague. The infection's cause was unknown, which increased panic in the city. It is now attributed to being bitten by fleas living on rats, and forensic evidence found on remains in London in 2014 indicates the disease was also spread by air, especially through coughs and sneezes.

Victims first suffered headaches followed by fever, chills, nausea and vomiting. The arms, legs and back became painful and hard, and intensely painful swellings appeared on the neck, under the arms and on the inner thighs, which began to ooze pus and blood. Death often came within three days of infection.

The city's population stood at some 80,000 and panic spread as up to 200 victims were buried each day between February and May. Londoners called it a scourge of God. The overcrowded city suffered from poor sanitation worsened by the plague deaths of all its street sweepers. The disease continued to rage until spring 1350 and is estimated to have killed one-third to one-half of London's population. Excavations have uncovered a mass grave at Spitalfields where corpses were stacked five deep. Among the victims were three Archbishops of Canterbury and the Abbot of Westminster Abbey, along with 27 of his monks.

There would be 16 more outbreaks, including the children's plague in 1361, before the Great Plague of 1665.

OPPOSITE: The skeletons of six plague victims were discovered buried in East Smithfield, London (under today's Royal Mint). A team of international scientists used DNA from the bones to find the entire genome of the plague.

'The streets were covered with the faeces of animals and people.'

London's Streets: Filth and Decay

Medieval Londoners endangered their health by merely walking outside. Streets were not paved and would become quagmires of mud and sewage. Special raised shoes were made to allow residents to walk above the filth, and residents placed low boards in the front door to hold back the muck and added rushes on the floors inside to clean their feet and shoes. The streets were covered with the faeces of animals and people, and estimates say this amounted to 50,000kg (50 tons) a day. Many residents emptied their chamber pots onto the street from upper windows, usually at night since such actions were illegal. The government hired muckrakers but this often created more of a stench. Residents and visitors also had to contend with the stink of offal, blood and rotting meat from animals

ABOVE: London's streets were quagmires of filth and disease too often inhabited by loud drunks and silent criminals. Law enforcement was weak or absent, so neighbours often had to rely on their own system of justice.

slaughtered in the street, all of which attracted the everyday swarms of rats that carried the plague bacillus. Only in 1369 were butchers banned from killing animals in the open air. Live animals also roamed freely, including pigs, geese, chickens and sheep. Adding to this stench were smells coming from various businesses, such as the tanneries that boiled leather. Londoners also regularly tossed out household rubbish despite the city scheduling a day for collections.

No relief came from the air. Outdoor burning mingled with the stench created a thick pollution that in 1285 caused Edward I to create the city's first commission on the problem. By the fifteenth century, however, the burning of coal made air quality even worse.

JOHN RYKENER

John Rykener was apprehended while wearing women's clothes on a London street near Cheapside during a December night in 1374 and having sex with another man. Calling himself Eleanor, he was taken to prison and appeared before London's aldermen for 'that detestable, unmentionable and ignominious crime.' He said women had taught him to cross-dress and then initiated him into prostitution. He worked as a prostitute in London, in Oxford for five weeks soliciting students and titled scholars, and then for six weeks in Burford where a Franciscan friar gave him a gold ring. He said several of his clients were priests, monks and nuns who all enjoyed his services for free. He also had sex as a man with women, many of them married. When he returned to London, he committed the vice with three chaplains in lanes by the Tower.

It is not known if he was officially charged or how his case ended. In the late medieval era in the city, at least 13 women were officially accused of dressing as men with their hair cut short.

Sin in the City

Medieval London was home to an array of criminals, from murderers to petty thieves, and both would be quickly hanged for their crimes, even youths. The winding streets that turned nearly invisible at night harboured prostitutes, vicious killers, knife-wielding robbers, pickpockets, vagrants and habitual drunks. Brazen thieves would be seen selling recently stolen goods on the neighbourhood streets. Rows of dismal, insignificant houses provided secret nests for brothels, criminal gangs and storage rooms full of stolen and blackmarket items. Even many respectable offices of business and government were prone to corruption, such as fraud, bribery and blackmail. This reached into the Guildhall in the 1380s when elections for mayor were swung by violence and even murder.

Prostitutes flourished throughout the city and were forbidden from dressing as 'good or noble dames or damsels.' The unlined hoods they wore had to be striped, and this became the identification of a prostitute. A concentration of brothels existed across the river in Southwark, ironically the seat of the Bishop of Winchester. In 1161, Henry II officially designated this borough as the site of 'stewhouses' or 'stews' (they were originally bathhouses) with the requirement of weekly inspections. The 'stewholders' were even placed under the direction of the bishop, who rented out most of the 'bathhouses.' By 1378, there were 18 establishments, all run by Flemish women. Besides the sexual pleasures, men could also enjoy food and drink as well as a scented bath.

London's authorities viewed brothels as a necessary evil, but not a criminal one unless their behaviour became unacceptable. Such a case in 1435 brought Peter Bednot into court to be fined for 'keeping a common brothel and receiving divers night-walking men.' Three years later, his wife Petronella was charged for having 'a stew within her house' in which 'she keeps divers malefactors, both thieves and common whores who turn away no one.'

BELOW: Street markets and fairs drew in large crowds whose shoppers were easy marks for sellers of stolen goods, pickpockets, thieves and prostitutes. The congested streets also increased the transmission of germs and diseases.

The Real Bedlam

Medieval London was not kind to the mentally ill. Bethlehem Royal Hospital, popularly known as Bedlam, was founded as a priory in 1247. It opened as a hospital around 1330 in Bishopsgate and added the first mental patients in 1403. Henry VIII gave it to the City of London in 1547 for use as a 'lunatic asylum.' The treatment proved to be more of a detention for the unfortunate patients that were sometimes called prisoners by their keepers. Some today would not be classified as insane, such as those who were epileptic, autistic or acutely melancholic. The criminally insane ranged from those accused of 'ruffianism' to murder, and a few were actually confined for political reasons.

Built over a sewer, the building's condition was filthy inside and out, where overflowing waste could block the entrance. By the time it moved to Moorfields in 1675, the staff had become infamous for their brutal treatment of patients and for charging the public to tour the facilities and gawk at the freak show. Visitors would laugh at the mistreated patients' antics and even poke them with sticks, returning home with graphic accounts of the lunatics' frightening cries, fights, curses and rattling of chains, for dangerous patients were chained to walls or locked in cells. Given pots for their bodily functions, they occasionally emptied their waste down on staff and visitors in the yard.

The name 'bedlam' has since been used to mean a noisy and confused place or situation. The hospital, in West Wickham since 1930, became part of the National Health Service as Bethlem Royal Hospital and specializes in research and treatment.

BELOW: Bedlam was a convenient place to isolate unwanted and elderly family members. It was not unknown for husbands who had tired of their wives to hand them over to the hospital along with a generous payment.

THE PLEASURE OF BLOOD

In medieval London, no amusement provided more wild excitement and bloodlust than the tormenting of animals. Cockfighting and dogfighting were common, but the most spectacular and grotesque blood sports were bullbaiting and bearbaiting.

Normally a Sunday afternoon event in a pit or arena, this popular entertainment was attended by all social classes. The bear or bull was chained by the neck or leg to a stake while vicious dogs, trained for the sport, harassed and attacked it, latching onto ears, neck and nose. Sometimes the animal was blinded and whipped for the performance or had pepper blown into its nose. Spectators bet on whether the baited animal would die during the torture that lasted about an hour.

Some bears had bloody careers that lasted for years, becoming popular heroes. Shakespeare mentioned one, Sackerson, in his *Merry Wives of Windsor*. Since bulls were more common, they were usually the victims and killed for meat if they survived the dogs. Butchers vowed that their meat was more tender due to the baiting.

ABOVE: Bearbaiting was so popular, Queen Elizabeth attended one event. London's most famous bear garden was located in Southwark.

ETATIS · · SVÆ · XLIX

THE TUDORS

The age of great sovereigns had arrived, and they ruled with unchecked power that defied the Church and subjected the masses, but also gave Londoners a more peaceful city and a blossoming culture that created Shakespeare.

Lᴏɴᴅᴏɴ's Tᴜᴅᴏʀ ᴇʀᴀ was dominated by their five sovereigns who strengthened the monarchy, established English colonies overseas with a dominant navy and created a new religious order. Three of their names stand out in the entire history of the monarchy: Henry VIII, Mary I ('Bloody Mary') and Elizabeth I ('the Virgin Queen').

The founder of the dynasty, Henry Tudor, was crowned as Henry VII in 1485 on the battlefield at Bosworth after his forces killed Richard III. Ever the peacemaker, he was able to unify the York and Lancaster dynasties, bringing their 85-year civil war to an end, and achieve another brief peace with Scotland. His son, Henry VIII, scandalized the Church and society by having six wives, beheading two and divorcing two. He also divorced the Roman Catholic Church to establish England's official Protestant religion that remains in place today. Mary I did bring back Catholicism and became known as 'Bloody Mary' in the process, which saw some 280 Protestants burned at the stake. The reign of her half-sister,

OPPOSITE: Later portraits of Henry VIII, such as this one by Hans Holbein when the King was 49, have left us with the image of a hefty, overweight monarch. When younger, Henry was a handsome athletic man who enjoyed sport.

Elizabeth I, re-established the Roman Church, but took a tolerant approach to religion. During her long reign of 45 years, she built England into a world power and oversaw voyages of discovery. She never married and her childless state ended the Tudor dynasty.

Peace, Prosperity and Panic

Compared to the trauma of the Middle Ages, the Tudor era brought more stability and wealth to the city and to much of England. John Aylmer, who would become Bishop of London in 1577, expressed a new national identity and patriotism in 1559 to his countrymen: 'Oh if thou knewst thou Englishmen in what wealth thou livest, and in how plentiful a country: Thou wouldest VII times a day fall flat on thy face before God and give him thanks that thou were born an Englishman, and not a French peasant, nor an Italian, nor German.'

A variety of new pleasures became available in town. Leisure time could be spent playing the new game of cards, which joined chess, draughts (checkers) and backgammon in the better homes. Entertainments in town were enjoyed by all social classes who could cross the river to still enjoy bullbaiting and bearbaiting (as Henry VIII and Elizabeth I did), or join the audience at the nearby Globe Theatre opened in 1599 to watch plays by William Shakespeare, Christopher Marlowe and Ben Jonson. More bawdy pleasures became available as well, with sexual misconduct not uncommon at the Royal court. In 1581, a 16-year-old Royal maid gave birth at Whitehall Palace after being seduced by the married Earl of Oxford. Queen Elizabeth was not amused, and they both ended up in the Tower.

Despite these advances, poverty was endemic among the swelling population that by 1605 had reached 75,000 within the city walls and another 150,000 in suburbs. Assessments for poor relief were already in place since

BELOW: Henry Tudor was crowned as Henry VII on Bosworth Field near Leicester after his victory ended the War of the Roses. Founding the Tudor dynasty, he was a peacemaker and modernized the nation's government.

1547 and almshouses and private charities provided more help, including grain distributions to the hungry.

Tudor England considered authority and order essential at all levels, from the state to the family. As the author Sir Thomas Elyot wrote in 1531, 'Take away order from things, what then should remain?' Such ideas were spread by England's first printing press, opened by William Claxton in 1476 in London's Westminster. A growing literacy and access to knowledge, however, created its own problems for the ruling class. In 1543, Henry VIII banned labourers, apprentices and even women from reading the newly translated English Bible.

Overlaying this were crises fermented by the crown. If there were heretics, it was because the Tudor rulers said there were. If residents of the city had become more civilized, their rulers had not. Henry VIII, who bore the title of 'Defender of the Faith' from the Pope, flew in the face of the Vatican in 1536 with his divorces and Dissolution of the Monasteries. Torture and capital punishment during Tudor days were extremely efficient and used more than in any other period. Henry VIII is estimated to have had 57,000 to 72,000 people executed, while 'Bloody' Mary burned about 280 Protestant men and women in less than five years.

As well as the fear of Royal authority, Tudor lives were always in danger of infections, diseases and epidemics. Tuberculosis, dysentery, influenza,

ABOVE: John Aylmer was proud to be an Englishman, but he was forced to live in exile in Europe during the reign of the Catholic Queen Mary. He returned when Queen Elizabeth restored the Protestant religion.

LEFT: William Caxton, shown here reading his proof sheets in Westminster Abbey, produced about 100 different items on his press. He printed everything from philosophy to popular literature, including Chaucer's *Canterbury Tales*.

WARBECK, THE PRETENDER

Pretenders to the throne seemed always available, and many had links by marriage, birth or foul play. Perkin Warbeck was different. Born in Tournai, Flanders, he lived in Portugal before travelling to Ireland in 1491 employed by a silk merchant. Impressed by Warbeck's silk clothes, Yorkist exiles convinced him to pretend to be Richard, Duke of York, the younger of the two princes in the Tower who had disappeared in 1483. Many believed he had escaped before his brother, Edward V, was murdered by Richard III. Warbeck went to Europe to raise an army and visit Margaret of Burgundy, the aunt of the real Richard who disappeared, and she trained him for the role. She publicly supported his claim, as did James IV of Scotland and Maximilian I of Austria, the Holy Roman Emperor.

In 1495 and 1496, Warbeck led invasions of England that failed. He then went to Scotland to marry Catherine Gordon, a cousin of James IV. He landed in Cornwall in 1497 to pronounce his claim on the throne as Richard IV. He was able to raise a force of 6000 men, but it was crushed by Henry VII's highly trained army at Exeter, preventing an overthrow of the first Tudor King. The pretender fled to Beaulieu, Hampshire, where he was captured and confessed to his deception. He was imprisoned in the Tower of London and, after an escape attempt, hanged in 1499 for plotting against the King, which was a humane death for such a crime.

LEFT: Five months before he was hanged at Tyburn, Perkin Warbeck was forced to make two public confessions at Westminster and Cheapside.

OPPOSITE: More than 100 spectators watched the clumsy beheading of Margaret Pole on Tower Green. Some still say they have seen her ghost in the Tower and that she re-enacts her execution on each anniversary of her death.

typhoid fever and small pox swept through the city. Elizabeth I survived a near fatal attack of the latter in 1562. Especially feared in the summer was the mysterious sweating sickness that could kill within hours, or as the contemporary historian Edward Hall noted, 'some merry at dinner and dead at supper.' The disease killed the wife and two daughters of Thomas Cromwell, Henry VIII's minister. Anne Boleyn, before she was Henry's second wife, survived a bout of 'the sweat' in 1538 along with her father and brother. Henry himself avoided crowds and constantly moved his court in 1517 to avoid this feared contagion.

Beheaded with 11 Blows

Margaret Pole was of the House of York that was defeated in 1485 at the Battle of Bosworth Field that brought Henry VII to the throne as the first Tudor King. Margaret's brother, Edward, the next York claimer to the throne, was executed in 1499 at the Tower of London, ending the Plantagenet rule of 14 monarchs.

Margaret fared better when the King arranged for her to marry Sir Richard Pole. After they had five children and her husband died in 1504, she had more luck five years later when Henry VIII ascended the throne and she was asked to attend Queen Catherine of Aragon. Her family's lands and titles were restored and Margaret became the wealthy Countess of Salisbury. Her life then went awry for supporting Catherine when her marriage to Henry was dissolved in 1533. Margaret was imprisoned in the Tower for two years and charged with treason as well as aiding and abetting her two sons who had spoken out against Henry.

She was executed at 7 a.m. on 27 May 1541. At the age of 67 and frail from illness, Margaret had to be dragged to the chopping block where she refused to place her head until forced. The axeman, who was young and inexperienced, blundered his way through the beheading as she struggled, first cutting into her shoulder and taking 11 swings to hack her head and shoulders to pieces. Another account said she escaped the executioner who cut her down as she ran.

> ## 'It took 11 swings to hack her head and shoulders to pieces.'

The Roman Catholic Church beatified Margaret as a martyr in 1886.

Henry VIII's Six Wives

The marital problems of Henry stemmed primarily from his desire for a son, but also from his unfaithful nature and the real or trumped-up adultery of his wives. Their fates, listed in a popular rhyme, were: 'divorced, beheaded, died, divorced, beheaded and survived.'

The 17-year-old King in 1509 wed Catherine of Aragon, his brother's widow who was five years older than him. The marriage ended in an annulment in 1533 to allow him to marry Anne Boleyn. Catherine died three years later. Their daughter became Queen Mary I.

Anne Boleyn married Henry secretly in 1533 while pregnant. He took a mistress that year and again the next. Anne produced a daughter (later becoming Queen Elizabeth I) and a stillborn son, so the King began to seek his freedom. In 1536, Henry accepted the confession of Mark Smeaton, one of Anne's musicians, that they had an affair – information that was obtained by his torture. Denying this, she was sent immediately to the Tower where she was accused of having four other lovers. All five men were executed on 17 May, and Anne herself two days later.

The day after Anne's beheading, Henry married Jane Seymour, one of Anne's maids who was known for her self-professed virtue. She gave Henry the son he desired on 12 October 1537, but she died 12 days later of fever. His son would become King Edward VI.

Anne of Cleves was summoned from the German duchy of that name to become Henry's fourth wife. He found her unattractive, said she smelled and doubted her virginity, but they were married on 6 January 1540. The marriage was unconsummated and a divorce followed in July.

Before his divorce, Henry had already pursued a maid of honour, Catherine Howard, the teenaged first cousin of Anne of Cleves. They were married in July 1540, the same month of his divorce. Word soon came to the King of Catherine's previous sexual activities, causing him to ask for a sword so he could kill her himself. An investigation also uncovered the Queen's new lover, Thomas Culpeper, a member of Henry's privy chamber. He, Catherine and her former lover Francis

OPPOSITE: Anne Boleyn, the mother of Elizabeth I, was the first of Henry VIII's wives to be beheaded. Once the King had decided to divorce or execute a wife, he was never affected by their appeals.

Dereham all went to the Tower. The two men were executed on 10 December 1541 and Catherine on 10 February 1542. The evening before her beheading, the Queen practised placing her head on the block so she would die with grace and dignity.

Henry's last wife, Catherine Parr, already twice widowed and childless, was somewhat unnerved by the fate of her husband's former wives. Married in 1543, she proved an admirable wife for the aging King, even serving as regent when he invaded France. After Henry's death in 1547, she wed Sir Thomas Seymour, the brother of Henry's third wife. The following year, she had her only child, but she died six days later.

The Nun of Kent

Elizabeth Barton, also known as the Holy Maid of Kent, was a simple woman and visionary who made prophesies that attacked Henry VIII's treatment of his wives. She was a domestic servant on an estate owned by William Warham, the Archbishop of Canterbury, located near Aldington, Kent. In 1525, when 19, Elizabeth experienced trances, including a vision of a nearby chapel. Taken there, she fell into a reverie that lasted a week, during which she raved and uttered mystical prophesies. Afterwards, pilgrims flocked to the small chapel. A monk allowed her to enter a Benedictine nunnery near Canterbury and her growing fame attracted yet more pilgrims.

Elizabeth's prophesies began to foretell dire consequences for Henry if he annulled his marriage to Catherine of Aragon and carried on with Anne Boleyn, saying he would no longer be King and 'should die a villain's death.' Cardinal Wolsey and Sir Thomas More had audiences with her and, such was Elizabeth's nerve, she confronted Henry during his visit to Canterbury and warned him of the dangers.

When Henry wed Anne, the nun continued to give virulent predictions about the King's future. The Archbishop of Canterbury, Thomas Cranmer, investigated. Elizabeth was arrested and confessed without torture to making up her trances and prophesies, and parliament condemned her and her sympathizers to death. They were taken to Tyburn on 21 April 1534, where Elizabeth was hanged and five priests were hanged, drawn and quartered. Sir Thomas More had been included in the charges, but produced a letter he supposedly wrote Elizabeth that warned against her meddling in Royal concerns.

'The evening before, the Queen practised placing her head on the block.'

Fatal Friendships

Wives were not the only ones endangered by their closeness to Henry VIII. Members of the court could go from trusted advisors to traitors overnight, moving from the palace to the Tower and worse. Three of Henry's favourites and best known throughout the country were Cardinal Wolsey, Thomas More and Thomas Cromwell, all of whom met unpleasant ends.

Thomas Wolsey, a butcher's son, became a cardinal and Henry's Lord Chancellor 'for life.' He had first become chaplain to the Archbishop of Canterbury and then to Henry VII. He rose rapidly when Henry VIII became King. He was made Archbishop of York in 1514 and cardinal a year later. Henry appointed him Lord Chancellor and from 1515 to 1529 Wolsey became a power behind the throne, given control of much of the state's administration and virtually in charge of foreign relations. He arranged an impressive meeting of Henry with Francis I, the King of France, from 7 to 24 June 1520 at the Field of Cloth of Gold near Calais, France. For all his tireless work, Wolsey became wealthy and built Hampton Court Palace 30km (19 miles) southwest of London. Yet at court, his arrogance and wealth made him generally disliked.

BELOW: The daughter of Sir Thomas More bid him farewell on the way to his execution. 'I die the King's faithful servant,' he said, 'but God's first.' The Roman Catholic Church later made him a saint.

Wolsey's downfall was strangely related to Henry's desire for a son. When the King decided to seek an annulment from Catherine of Aragon, who had produced a daughter, Wolsey was put in charge of securing this from the Pope. Despite his influence, he failed and Henry was furious, having him charged with taking orders from a foreign power: the Pope. Henry took Hampton Court for his own when it was completed in 1526 and would not allow Wolsey near him, sending him four years later to his diocese of York. The cardinal was arrested for treason by the Earl of Northumberland in the market town of Cawood near York and died on 29 November 1530 while returning to London (with his legs tied to his horse) for his trial. A rumour said he had taken poison to avoid being beheaded.

Sir Thomas More had a privileged life. The son of a London lawyer and judge, he studied at Oxford and became a lawyer. Intellectual and serious, he was an under-sheriff of London in 1510 and a personal advisor to Henry in 1517, serving as his secretary and chief diplomat. He was knighted in 1521, became speaker of the House of Commons two years later and chancellor of the Duchy of Lancaster in 1525. More published *Utopia* in 1516, describing an ideal land where reason ruled.

He passionately supported the Roman Catholic Church to the point of interrogating heretics and causing some to be burned at the stake. When Henry broke with Rome to become supreme head of the Church in England, More resigned as chancellor and opposed the annulment of the King's marriage to Catherine of Aragon. More, very religious and moral, refused to attend the coronation of her replacement, Anne Boleyn. Royal commissioners summoned him on April 1534 to take an oath assenting to the Act of Succession that declared Henry's marriage valid. More did agree that Anne was Queen, but refused the oath because it declared Henry as head of the Church in England instead of the Pope. He was imprisoned in the Tower on 17 April and remained there until his trial for treason the following year on 1 July. The judges, who included Anne's father, brother and nephew, unanimously found him guilty. More was sentenced to be hanged, drawn and quartered, but Henry changed this to beheading. This happened on Tower Hill on 6 July. More asked to be taken up safely to the scaffold 'and for my coming down, let me shift for myself.' Instead of the usual procedure, he blindfolded himself to play his own part in the drama.

Thomas Cromwell came to an equally bad end, even though he successfully oversaw the Reformation and dissolution of the monasteries. Born the son of a brewer and blacksmith in Putney near London, Cromwell spent time in Europe, but little is known about his early life. His importance grew in 1520 when he became solicitor to Cardinal Wolsey who sent him five years later to direct the dissolution of some smaller monasteries. After Wolsey's fall, Cromwell entered parliament. In 1530, he was chosen by Henry as a member of his council and the following year became one of his confidential advisors. In 1534, he secured the Act of Supremacy that made Henry head of the Church instead of the Pope. In 1539, he became the Lord Great Chamberlain and the next year was created Earl

ABOVE: Sir Thomas Cromwell was a brilliant lawyer and before his downfall was one of the King's most skilful advisors. He suffered the personal tragedies of his wife and two daughters dying in 1528 from the 'sweating sickness.'

'He blindfolded himself to play his own part in the drama.'

of Essex. The King appointed him vicar-general to carry out the Dissolutions of the Monasteries, and by 1540 Cromwell had closed them all.

Despite these triumphs, he faced a conspiracy led by Thomas Howard, the Duke of Norfolk, who disliked the rise of this commoner and the way he dominated the court. Cromwell created his own trouble by pushing for a wider type of Protestantism and links with Lutherans. Norfolk and other enemies passed an anti-Protestant act in 1539. Cromwell made things worse by orchestrating the King's marriage in 1540 to Anne of Cleves, a union that proved a fiasco and publicly humiliated Henry, who divorced her after six months. Cromwell was arrested for heresy and treason on 10 June 1540 and condemned without a hearing. He was

'Cromwell's head was boiled and displayed on a spike on London Bridge.'

beheaded in the Tower on 28 July, the day Henry married Catherine Howard. It took the young axeman three strokes, and rumour said Henry had purposely chosen an inexperienced executioner who was 'a ragged and butcherly miser.' Cromwell's head was boiled and displayed on a spike on London Bridge.

Beheading the Teenaged Queen

Lady Jane Grey became Queen in 1553 at the death of Edward VI. His half-sister, Mary, was next in line, but the Protestant Duke of Northumberland persuaded the dying King to exclude her because she was Catholic. Edward declared her and another half-sister, Elizabeth, as illegitimate. Northumberland then gained the crown for 16-year-old Lady Jane Grey, the great-granddaughter of Henry II and married to Northumberland's son, Guildford Dudley. When told she was Queen, Jane fainted and had to be strongly persuaded before accepting the title.

Her reign lasted nine days until Mary and her supporters marched on London intent on continuing the Tudor dynasty. Even Jane's father, the Duke of Suffolk, shifted his support to Mary and persuaded his daughter to give up her crown, which she willingly did, saying she had only been following her parents'

BOILED IN OIL

During Henry VIII's reign, parliament passed a terrifying method of execution for poisoners who would be boiled in oil like a traitor. The first unfortunate victim was Richard Roose, the cook of John Fisher, Bishop of Rochester. Roose attempted to kill his employer by adding poisonous powder to the common pot of porridge to be served at dinner to the family, guests and servants. The bishop was not hungry, but the fatal meal was eaten by others, resulting in two deaths – a gentleman in the household and a destitute widow – and leaving several more with lifelong illnesses. When Roose was arrested, he said he thought he was adding a laxative as a practical jest, but he was found guilty without a trial by the King's order.

On 5 April 1531, Roose was boiled to death in a cauldron at London's Smithfield where he was locked into a chain and pulled in and out of the boiling liquid by a gibbet until dead. Witnesses said 'he roared mighty loud.'

John Fisher, the surviving bishop, fell out with Henry over his marriage to Anne Boleyn. He was beheaded on 22 June 1535 on Tower Hill and his head displayed on Tower Bridge.

STOCKS AND PILLORY

Tudor punishments for minor crimes involved humiliation rather than torture and death. Two popular forms, being locked into the stocks and the pillory, did seem like minor torture to the victims. The stocks consisted of a hinged wooden board with holes through which the prisoner's legs were held and locked into place. The pillory was a variation on this, with a hinged wooden board raised on one or two poles with holes for the head and hands to be locked in, causing the criminal to stand. Both were normally situated in a very public place, such as a market, to allow people to laugh, punch, spit or hurl abuse at the prisoner. They also hurled rotten food and worse.

Offenders often seen in these devices ranged from ruffians to prostitutes. In 1488, Christine Houghton was convicted of being 'a common bawd and common strumpet' and ordered out of London. When she came back, she was given two hours in a pillory followed by a prison sentence of one year and a day.

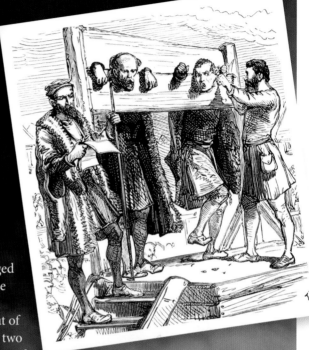

ABOVE: The pillory had the extra discomfort of forcing prisoners to stand and be vulnerable to slaps and kicks on their bottoms.

LEFT: Stocks were also used to hold defendants for hours before their court appearances. The cruel device was discontinued in 1872.

Paul Delaroche's famous oil painting of Lady Jane Grey's execution is displayed in London's National Gallery. The executioner held up her severed head and said, 'So perish all the Queen's enemies. Behold the head of a traitor.'

wishes. The new Queen pardoned Dorset and promised mercy for Jane, but the young girl pleaded guilty and was condemned along with her husband to die for treason. Mary suspended Jane's sentence, but reinstated it after her father's part in Sir Thomas Wyatt's rebellion in February 1554. Mary made another effort to save Jane, sending the Dean of St Paul's to persuade her to become Catholic, but she refused.

Jane watched from her window in the Tower as her husband Guildford Dudley was beheaded at 10 a.m on the morning of 12 February. After his body was taken to the chapel, she was led an hour later to a block within the Tower. Wearing black and carrying a prayer book, she gave a last speech to the small gathering, saying others had sinned against Mary in her name, so 'I do wash my hands thereof in innocency, before God and the face of you good Christian people today.' After reciting the 51st Psalm, she began to untie her outer gown. The masked executioner stepped forward to receive it (since it would become his property) and she stepped back startled and told him to leave her alone. 'I pray you dispatch me quickly,' she told him. Jane gave her gloves to her ladies and was blindfolded. Unable to see, she fumbled to find the block, asking 'What shall I do? Where is it?' After being guided to it, she exclaimed, 'Lord, into thy hands I commend my spirit!' and was then beheaded with one stroke. Her father, who had been caught hiding in a hollow tree, was executed two days later.

> **'Wyatt was imprisoned in the Tower and tortured without success.'**

Wyatt's Rebellion

The planned marriage of Mary Tudor to Prince Philip of Spain, thereby returning England to Catholicism, provoked a conspiracy to depose Mary in favour of her half-sister, Princess Elizabeth. Four uprisings were planned in Herefordshire, Leicestershire (led by the father of imprisoned Lady Jane Grey), the Southwest and Kent. The latter was to be led by Sir Thomas Wyatt the Younger. Their plan was to wed Elizabeth to Edward Courtenay, a descendant of Edward IV, but Edward repaid the compliment by informing Queen Mary. The other three leaders had no success raising their forces, but Wyatt was not deterred. He gave a rallying speech four days later on 25 January 1554 in Maidstone, Kent, where he said the rebellion was not so much against the Queen as a 'quarrel against Strangers,' the Spanish who would be lured to England after the union.

Mary immediately ordered an army under the Duke of Norfolk to pursue Wyatt and put down the revolt, but the Duke failed to engage him in battle and virtually joined Wyatt.

Wyatt's army of some 3000 men began its move on London. Mary gave her own rallying call, telling a large crowd that her council had advised her to complete the marriage, but that her first marriage was to her people and the Common Weal. This galvanized Londoners to lock the city gates and defend London Bridge by the time Wyatt's force arrived on 3 February. Instead, he crossed Kingston Bridge and reached Hyde Park and Ludgate on 7 February, striking fear into the city's population. Mary was urged to flee, but told her court to pray, assuring them of God's protection.

She was right. Wyatt's men became disorganized and undisciplined as Londoners failed to support their cause, and the Royal army moved in to capture their leader. Wyatt was imprisoned in the Tower and tortured without success to

OPPOSITE: After Wyatt's execution, those opposed to Queen Mary Tudor regarded him and his men as martyrs. Wyatt was the grandfather of Francis Wyatt, who became the first Royal Governor of the colony of Virginia.

ABOVE: Princess Elizabeth entered the Tower through the Traitors' Gate. The water gate was built by Edward I as his entrance to St Thomas's Tower, but later received its name from the traitors conveyed there in barges.

implicate Elizabeth in the plot. Taken to be beheaded, he tied his own blindfold and said no other person then held in the Tower, which included Elizabeth, 'was privy to my rising.' This may have saved her life, for she was only imprisoned for two months.

Nearly 100 of Wyatt's men were executed and mutilated and later displayed throughout the city, but Queen Mary paroled most of the traitors.

How Bloody was Mary?

Mary, the daughter of Henry VIII and Catherine of Aragon, remained a devout Catholic, along with her mother, after Henry replaced the Pope as head of the English church. When Henry wed Anne Boleyn and they had a daughter, Elizabeth, an act of parliament declared Mary illegitimate and removed her from the line of succession. She was reinstated in 1544 after she recognized Henry as head of the church. When Edward I, her Protestant 16-year-old brother died, he had named Lady Jane Grey as his successor, but supporters of Mary overthrew the 'Nine-Day Queen' and orchestrated her beheading despite the new Queen's regret.

Mary's first act on taking the throne in 1553 was to reinstate Catholicism. Her planned marriage to her cousin Phillip II, heir to the Spanish throne, would consolidate the religion. Parliament opposed this and unrest broke out, such as Wyatt's Rebellion, but the wedding took place in 1554 and Mary had him declared King of England. She was 38 and he 26.

Now Mary returned the church to the Pope's authority, ordered mass to be conducted at court and throughout London and revived the heresy laws that required anyone not Catholic to be burned at the stake. The Queen used her full power against 'heretic' Protestants, earning her the nickname of 'Bloody Mary'. Among those burned were Archbishop of Canterbury Thomas Cranmer and the bishops Hugh Latimer and Nicholas Ridley. As many as 280 Protestants are estimated to have been killed during her reign.

For his part, Phillip returned to Spain after only 14 months. He became King and their marriage drew England into war with France. In January 1558, Calais was lost, which was England's last possession across the Channel. Mary, who had no children (and suffered two false pregnancies), died later that year at the age of 42.

ABOVE: Philip II, King of Spain, and his wife, Queen Mary I, in an official procession. Mary was 12 years older, and her husband had early doubts about the marriage arranged by Charles V, Philip's father and Mary's cousin.

Thomas Cranmer

Born in Nottinghamshire, Thomas Cranmer attended Cambridge and became a priest in 1533. Henry VIII met him in Essex, where Cranmer had retreated from the plague. Finding that the young man advocated the King's divorce from Catherine of Aragon, Henry included him in the delegation sent in 1530 to argue the case in Rome. Two years later he made him ambassador to the Holy Roman Emperor in Germany, with the idea he would investigate Lutheranism. While there, Cranmer wed the niece of a Lutheran reformer. He had to hide this until made the first Protestant Archbishop of Canterbury in 1533. It was Cranmer who declared Henry's marriage to Catherine void. He conducted the King's marriage to Anne Boleyn, but later invalidated it due to her supposed adultery. He also helped Henry divorce Anne of Cleves and took a major part in proceedings that led to the execution of Catherine Howard.

Following Henry's death and the succession of Edward VI, Cranmer worked in 1549 on the Church's new *Book of Common Prayer*, having already pushed to have the Bible translated into English. He then made a key mistake in supporting Lady Jane Grey's claim to the throne on Edward's death. When Mary became Queen in 1553 and reinstated Catholicism, she had Cranmer tried for treason. He signed six recantations, admitted his error in supporting Protestantism and recognized the Pope as head of the Church. He was nevertheless sentenced to be burned on 21 March 1556 in Oxford, where he had already been forced to watch from a tower while the Bishops Hugh Latimer and Nicholas Ridley died in the same matter.

'Nearly 100 of Wyatt's men were executed and mutilated and later displayed throughout the city.'

The Other Oxford Martyrs

Thomas Cranmer was the high profile victim of Queen Mary's war on Protestants, but the other two Oxford martyrs, Hugh Latimer and Nicholas Ridley, provided brave inspiration as well. They were burned together five months before Cranmer. Today, the huge Martyrs' Memorial, completed in 1843, stands in Oxford close to the site of wasteland outside the city's north gate where the three died. A small cobblestone cross is also set in the middle of Broad Street at the actual site.

Hugh Latimer, the son of a Leicestershire farmer, attended Cambridge and was ordained a Catholic priest around 1510. He converted to Protestantism in 1525 and gave public support for King Henry's desire to annul his marriage to Catherine of Aragon. The King heard him preach in 1530 and appointed him Royal chaplain, but he was excommunicated and imprisoned two years later for speaking against the existence of purgatory and the veneration of saints.

RIGHT: Hugh Latimer and Nicholas Ridley were burned together before a large crowd in Oxford. They and Thomas Cranmer had been tried in Oxford's University Church of St Mary the Virgin and were immediately declared guilty.

The Martyrdom of Dr Rid
Dr Smith Preaching

Thomas Cromwell, the King's chief minister, helped Latimer become the Bishop of Worcester in 1535, and he became a leading advocate for reform. Some of his ideas landed him in the Tower, but he recovered under the stronger Protestantism that was allowed after the accession of the young Edward VI. His sermons on Reformation attracted large congregations and approval by the court.

This was his undoing when Mary Tudor became Queen and set about executing the most influential Protestants. Latimer, who had supported the Protestant Queen, Lady Jane Grey, was arrested on treason charges, tried in Oxford, found guilty and burned at the stake, bound by an iron chain to another well-known reformer, Nicholas Ridley, on 16 October 1555. As they were

'Thomas Cranmer was the high profile victim of Queen Mary's war on Protestants.'

Mr Latimer at OXFORD,
ime of their Suffering.

bound together and a lighted
faggot placed at Ridley's
feet, Latimer gained fame by
encouraging Ridley, who was
some 15 years younger, by
urging, 'Be of good comfort,
Master Ridley, and play the
man. We shall this day light
such a candle by God's grace
in England as I trust shall
never be put out.'

Nicholas Ridley was
born in Northumberland
and, like Hugh Latimer, was
educated at Cambridge and
became a priest around 1534.
After studying in France, he
returned to Cambridge and
was a leader of the Reformist
movement that would
influence Protestantism.
After serving as canon of
Canterbury and Westminster,
he became Bishop of
Rochester and in 1550
Bishop of London, having
worked on producing the
new *Book of Common Prayer*.
Following Reformist ideas, he
infamously replaced the altar
with a table for communion
and denied the Catholic doctrine of transubstantiation that said the communion
bread becomes Christ's body.

Like Latimer, Ridley supported Lady Jane Grey as Queen and was immediately
arrested for treason after the accession of the Catholic Queen, Mary I. Quickly
condemned, he was burned together with Hugh Latimer on 16 October 1555.
Latimer seemed to die with little pain, but Ridley suffered because the lighted
faggots under him were green and burned the lower half of his body. His brother-
in-law and another man poked the faggots to increase the flames and hasten
death, and Ridley died from the explosion of a bag of gunpowder tied around his
neck (placed by his brother, who also gave some to Latimer).

The Virgin Queen

With the death of Queen Mary in 1558, the crown passed to the daughter of
Henry III and Anne Boleyn, whom he executed. Elizabeth I came to the throne
unmarried and needed to produce an heir to continue the Tudor reign. For this
reason, Members of Parliament were unnerved when she first addressed them in
1559 and ended by saying her future tomb would be inscribed, 'Here lies interred
Elizabeth, a virgin pure until her death.' Among her numerous suitors was Philip
of Spain, who hoped to have England remain Catholic.

TORTURERS OF THE TOWER

Two names stand out among those who inflicted torture in the Tower of London during Elizabeth's reign. Thomas Norton was a member of parliament's House of Commons who was assigned to interrogate Catholic prisoners, and became feared as 'Norton the Rackmaster' and even 'The Rackmaster-General.'

The most sadistic torturer was said to be Richard Topcliffe, also in the House of Commons, who preferred hanging his victims off the ground in manacles. He put his prisoner Anne Bellamy on the rack in another prison until she betrayed 26 people, including her parents, and then raped her. Topcliffe was also known to torture victims in his own house.

Elizabeth I would be a cautious Queen who seemed to return her country to Protestantism without ruthless revenge, but rather by reversing Mary's laws that established the Roman Church. Elizabeth had allowed mass at the funeral of Mary, but several bishops turned down the opportunity to preside at her coronation, worried about the future. It came in 1559 with passage of the Act of Supremacy that made Elizabeth head of a Protestant state religion. She was excommunicated by the Pope, but England's fervent Catholics had no plans to desert their religion. By 1584, a Catholic priest could be tried for treason and three years later anyone attending Protestant church services could be fined £260.

The Queen and her people also confronted large outbreaks of disease. During her reign, the plague struck five times. In 1592 and 1593, she ordered all theatres closed, which stopped the run of Shakespeare's *Henry VI* at the Rose Theatre. Particularly virulent were the plagues of 1563 and 1603, each time reducing London's population by more than a quarter. Elizabeth was terrified as up to 1800 people died each week. She moved her court to Windsor Castle in 1563 where she had a gallows erected with orders to hang anyone arriving from London. Other prevalent diseases included smallpox, which the Queen had at the age of 29, typhus, syphilis and ague (malaria).

'She had a gallows erected with orders to hang anyone arriving from London.'

The Spanish Armada

The greatest troubles of Elizabeth's reign were the plots of Catholics and their persecution, yet her most glorious triumph came against an invading Catholic force, the Spanish Armada. King Philip sent it in 1588 to restore that religion to England because he was furious over attacks by Sir Francis Drake on Spanish ships in 1585 and 1586 in the Caribbean. Even earlier, Drake had circumnavigated the world, returning in 1580 with treasure from the Spanish ships he attacked. Elizabeth knighted him the next year. When news of the the Armada's preparations reached England, Drake raided Spanish ships in Cadiz harbour in 1587, destroying some 30 and saying he was 'singeing the beard of the King of Spain.'

In May 1588, the Armada of some 150 ships sailed from Lisbon carrying about 19,000 soldiers and 8000 sailors. The Duke of Medina-Sidonia commanded the

Ships of the Armada were sunk near the shores of Scotland and Ireland. Archaeologists examining the wrecks have found a lack of care with the equipment that would have caused confusion among the crews.

fleet that had 40 or so ships armed for heavy battle. The English fleet also had some 40 warships among 66 vessels, but put their reliance on more heavy guns and fewer soldiers, as well as their ships being faster than the Armada's. It was commanded by Charles Howard, Baron Howard of Effingham, with Sir Francis Drake as vice admiral, second in command.

Severe gales forced the Armada back to a port in northern Spain, and it began again on 12 July (old style calendar), being first sighted off Cornwall on the 19th heading for the English Channel while the English ships were being resupplied in Plymouth harbour. In three engagements from Plymouth to the Isle of Wight, the superior English guns kept the Spanish from closing in to allow their better-equipped army to board. Neither side suffered major damage. On 27 July, the Armada anchored off Calais, France, with plans to clear the Strait of Dover and wait for an army of 30,000 men headed by the Duke of Parma, the Spanish regent of the Netherlands. His ships took six days to arrive, and meanwhile at midnight at the end of 7 August, Drake sent eight unmanned fire ships into the Armada that had to cut anchors and scatter in all directions.

At dawn the next day, the English attacked off Gravelines, France, and inflicted a defeat using their superior guns. Four of the enemy's ships were sunk or driven onto land and others badly disabled. Shifting winds and the English fleet prevented any chance of Parma's Netherlands army crossing the Channel. The Armada had to return to Spain around the northern tip of Scotland. Low on ammunition and supplies, the English turned back, leaving the damaged Armada to battle harsh weather and unsure navigation. Only six ships returned safely to Spain. Estimated deaths totalled about 15,000 for Spain and 1000 or less for England, of which many were due to disease.

After this, her greatest victory, Elizabeth appeared in public with her troops and won praise and admiration from her people.

RIGHT: Queen Elizabeth joined her troops at the port of Tilbury in Essex when the Armada was approaching England, and she later celebrated the Spanish defeat by riding out again in public with the troops.

FRANCIS DRAKE GOES BOWLING

The story was told that Francis Drake was playing a game of lawn bowls with his officers when informed that the Spanish Armada had been sighted, and he insisted there was ample time to both win his game and beat the Spaniards. Some believe Drake knew his ships in Plymouth Harbour could not immediately leave port because of the tide. The game was being played on the city's large open green space, Plymouth Hoe (meaning 'high place') on limestone cliffs over the seafront. Drake supposedly lost the game, but won the war.

Bowls have been played on that green for 500 years.

LEFT: No eyewitness accounts were ever recorded of Drake's game, but the heroic story persists and has never been disproved.

The Earl of Leicester

Despite some effort, research has never revealed that Elizabeth had a consummated love affair. Perhaps her greatest love was Robert Dudley, the Earl of Leicester. In 1553, he joined his father in supporting Lady Jane Grey's elevation to the throne and was condemned to death. Pardoned the following year, he went with his brother to fight in France. His good fortune came when the new Queen Elizabeth appointed him as her Master of the Horse. He quickly became her consort and confidant. His wife, married when he was 18, died suddenly in 1560, and suspicions abounded that he murdered her with the intention of marrying Elizabeth, who would openly tease and flirt with him. She gave him land and many other rewards, naming him Protector of the Realm in case of her death. Dudley informed Spanish ambassadors he would return England to Catholicism if Philip II would help arrange the wedding.

'Estimated deaths totalled about 15,000 for Spain and 1000 or less for England.'

All this came to an end when Elizabeth encouraged Dudley to wed her rival, Mary Queen of Scots. Still, she kept him as her favourite, calling him 'my eyes' and elevating him to Earl of Leicester in 1564, the same year Dudley was named

chancellor of Oxford University. 'I stand at the top of the hill,' he wrote in 1566. His influence also sent a few of his enemies to the scaffold. In 1578, Dudley married a widow, Lady Essex, making him the stepfather of Robert Devereux, Elizabeth's next court favourite.

Dudley's star began to wane when the Queen had him lead an army to the Netherlands in 1585 to assist their fight with Spain. He spent much time enjoying himself and doing little about fighting the Spaniards. She recalled him in 1587 and gave him command of troops in Tilbury in August 1588 to resist any possible Spanish invasion. He remained by her side during the Spanish Armada battles and died suddenly as the defeated Armada was in retreat. Elizabeth shut herself in her chambers after receiving news of his death, and her council had the door broken down days later. Even then, she could not carry on duties for some time. She treasured Robert's final letter in which he wrote: 'I humbly kiss your foot,' and kept it in a box on her table, adding 'his last letter' across it.

A Fatal Attraction

Another of Elizabeth's court favourites was Robert Devereux, the Earl of Essex, which for him would also prove a fatal attraction. His father had been a favourite of the Queen, and in her later years Elizabeth felt the same love for Robert, a handsome hero who had fought the Spanish in the Netherlands in 1586. They danced together and would play cards into the early morning. She favoured him with appointments at court where the two of them were known for their close relationship that alternated between devoted love and furious disagreements.

Robert Devereux began to take the Queen's love for granted. He disobeyed her in 1589 by joining the English Armada a year after it had defeated the Spanish Armada. Even worse, he began

THE BARD AND THE QUEEN

Despite the early clash of religions in Elizabeth's 44-year reign, she left England more powerful and secure. Londoners found time to enjoy the blossoming of entertainment and culture. Playhouses were especially popular, offering intelligent dramas written and performed by William Shakespeare, Christopher Marlowe, Richard Burbage and others. Although she never attended a theatre, Queen Elizabeth was a devoted supporter, being the patron of her own company, the Queen's Men. She invited actors many times to give special court performances. Shakespeare and his company, the Lord Chamberlain's Men, played before her at her palaces in Richmond and Greenwich. Elizabeth became such a patron of Shakespeare that she influenced his writing. When she requested a play featuring the fat comic character Falstaff in love, the Bard wrote *The Merry Wives of Windsor*. The Queen even had Shakespeare change the character's name from the original Oldcastle to Falstaff to avoid offending members of the Oldcastle family.

When Elizabeth died, Shakespeare praised her in *King Henry VIII*, saying she would die 'yet a virgin; A most unspotted lily shall she pass to the ground, and all the world will mourn her.'

RIGHT: In the last decade of her life, Queen Elizabeth had Shakespeare's company perform at court three times each year.

to fail. His effort to attack the Spanish treasure ships off the Azores in 1590 went badly and, after appointed Lord Lieutenant of Ireland, he was not successful in putting down a 1599 rebellion there, only securing an unofficial truce. Having survived on his charm, Devereux could not survive Elizabeth's humiliation. She took away his official duties and put him under house arrest. His miscalculated response on 8 February 1601 was to lead a force of more than 100 armed men from the Strand to the City, futilely calling on Londoners to revolt. This last failure led to his trial and he was beheaded for treason at the age of 34 on 25 February. He requested a private execution, which was granted on the Tower of London's courtyard. Elizabeth was playing the virginal harpsichord at court when informed of his death. She paused for a moment, said nothing and began playing again.

OPPOSITE: Although a favourite of Queen Elizabeth, Robert Devereux's relationship with her was uneasy. One of his worse moments came when he faced an Irish rebellion in 1599 and made an unofficial truce that infuriated Elizabeth.

ANNO. DÑI ÆTATIS SVÆ 21

1585

QVOD ME NVTRIT
ME DESTRVIT

Was Marlowe Murdered?

Christopher Marlowe was a towering figure in the Elizabethan theatre, writing such classics as *The Jew of Malta* and *Edward II*. He influenced Shakespeare and other contemporary playwrights, and suspicions remain that he wrote some of the Bard's plays. He was also a poet who established blank verse.

Marlowe was born the same year as Shakespeare, 1564, and studied at Cambridge. The two knew each other by 1591 at London's Rose Theatre, where Marlowe's works were performed. The written word could be dangerous in those days of religious persecution. Some believed that Marlowe's *Edward II* about a King's weakness for favourites was meant to be a reflection of Elizabeth. Thomas Kyd, the author of *The Spanish Tragedy*, was arrested in 1593 for heresy and died from torture. At his home, authorities found notes mentioning Marlowe as a possible source for Kyd's works. That year, Marlowe, despite being a secretly paid government agent, was arrested twice, interrogated by the Privy Council and accused of being pro-Catholic (although an apparent atheist) and then released.

On 30 May 1593, Marlowe and three other state spies, including Robert Poley, an agent provocateur, met at a government safe house in Deptford. In the evening a quarrel broke out and Ingram Frizer stabbed Marlowe above his right eye, killing him instantly. Authorities accepted the story that the argument was over a bill and a jury decided the killer acted in self-defence after Marlowe had grabbed Frizer's dagger and wounded him on the head. Frizer was pardoned, and suspicions arose and remained that the government had the outspoken playwright assassinated.

Mary, Queen of Scots

Mary was the only child of James V of Scotland. She was six days old when he died, and her French mother served as regent. At the age of five, Mary was engaged to Edward, the son of Henry VIII, but her Catholic protectors reneged on the agreement and betrothed her to the heir to the French crown, Francis, who was only four. They were wed in 1558, and he became King the next year. However, he died in 1560 and Mary, at the age of 18, returned from the French court.

Although a Catholic in Protestant Scotland, Mary did nothing to force her religion on her subjects. In 1565, she married the Englishman, Henry Stuart, Earl of Darnley, her cousin, and their marriage fared poorly. The next year he and a group of Protestant nobles burst into Mary's chambers as she was having supper

OPPOSITE: This portrait, discovered in 1952 at Corpus Christi College, Cambridge, is believed to be of Christopher Marlowe. He was 29 when murdered and was staying in Kent at the time to avoid the plague in London.

BELOW: Mary's second husband, Henry Stuart, Lord Darnley, was an arrogant man who tried to rule with her and become absolute King if he outlived her. When he was apparently murdered, some suspected Mary may have been involved.

with six friends. They forced her Italian secretary, David Rizzio, into an adjoining room, accusing him of having an affair with the Queen, and stabbed him 56 times as he clung to Mary's skirts. The Queen was pregnant at the time, and their son, James, was born in 1566. The following year, Darnley was involved in an explosion when living in Kirk o' Field, Edinburgh, and, although unscathed by the blast, he was found strangled. Three months later Mary wed the chief suspect, the Earl of Bothwell, who was soon banished by a rebellion that in 1567 forced Mary to abdicate. Her son was made King and she was imprisoned, but she escaped the next year to rally an army. When it was defeated near Glasgow, Mary fled to England seeking protection from Elizabeth, arriving unexpectedly on 17 May 1586.

'15 minutes after the sword fell, witnesses said her lips were moving as if in prayer.'

This was a wrong move. Elizabeth distrusted her Catholic cousin, never met with her and had her imprisoned. This created several Catholic plots to rescue Mary and place her on the English throne. One involved Elizabeth's cousin, Thomas Howard, Duke of Norfolk, who hoped to wed Mary. He was discovered and sent to the Tower where he was executed in 1572. Mary then made the mistake of corresponding with another plotter, Anthony Babington, who was arranging to kill the Queen. When his letters were intercepted by one of the monarch's spies, Mary denied any knowledge, but Elizabeth had her tried for treason. Mary was given the death sentence in October 1586 and beheaded at Fotheringhay Castle in Northamptonshire on 8 February 1587. About 15 minutes after the sword fell, witnesses said her lips were moving as if in prayer.

Ironically, Mary's son succeeded Elizabeth in 1603 as James I, the first Stuart King.

RIGHT: Mary Stuart suffered the trauma of being present when her husband took part in the murder of David Rizzio in an adjoining room. The Earl of Bothwell was also a target, but escaped through a window.

Priest Holes

When Elizabeth began persecutions of Catholics, their priests were placed in mortal danger. None were allowed to enter the country, and the Queen sent out 'priest hunters' to identify and arrest those that remained who would then be tried for treason. Some Catholic families, especially those with large country houses, were willing to hide priests at much risk to themselves. The fugitives sometimes posed as family members or teachers, but the safest option was a hidden space that became known as a priest hole. Owners of a safe house, often marked with a secret symbol, would seal off or have a small space built that allowed a priest to hide when the hunters or authorities visited. The claustrophobic areas were often in the attic, under floorboards or behind a false fireplace. If the raiding parties made extensive searches of the area for days, a hidden priest might suffer from hunger and thirst or in some cases die. One Jesuit, Father Richard Blount, had to hide behind a stone wall as the house was searched for 10 days. He and a companion survived on a loaf of bread and a bottle of wine. Father Blount later became head of the Jesuit English Mission.

The most active and best builder of priest holes was Nicholas Owen. Born in Oxford, he followed in his father's profession and became a carpenter. He was finally captured in 1594 and tortured, but refused to reveal hiding places or names. Owen was released after a ransom was paid and went back to building priest holes. In 1597, he also arranged an amazing escape of two Jesuit priests from the Tower. He was starved out of hiding in Worcestershire and re-arrested in 1605 after James I assumed the throne. Owen, responsible for saving many lives over some 20 years, was taken to the Tower and on 2 March 1606 died hanging from a rack that caused his intestines to burst from an old hernia. The Catholic Church canonized him in 1970.

ABOVE: Priest holes were built around the country, and some houses had two or three. Visitors can see priest holes today at National Trust properties, such as the one where King Charles II hid at Moseley Old Hall in Staffordshire.

SEVENTEENTH CENTURY

A series of disasters tested the hearts of Londoners. Royalty's rule was lost and regained, many lives were taken by the plague and the city itself was almost destroyed in a blazing inferno that was started in a bakery.

ELIZABETH'S LONG REIGN brought continuity and stability, but the era of Stuart Kings proved to be a whirlwind of changes and rulers. Londoners saw their King beheaded, the nation turned into a commonwealth and Royalty returned before the Stuarts were swept aside by the 'Glorious Revolution.'

Union and Turmoil
James I had a frantic childhood and youth, surrounded by intrigue, war and murder. As a claimant on the throne, he was lucky to have survived. He became King of Scotland when his mother, Mary, abdicated in 1567, although regents ruled until 1576. With hopes of succeeding Queen Elizabeth, he formed an alliance with her in 1585 and hardly protested two years later when she executed his Catholic mother. When Elizabeth died in 1603, James took the English crown, becoming the first monarch to unite the two countries. Although a Protestant and head of the Presbyterian Church in Scotland, James was regarded

OPPOSITE: London's most spectacular tragedy of the Seventeenth century was the great fire that raged for four days. It forced the population to save themselves and as many possessions as possible, with many taken to the Thames.

with suspicion by many of his subjects. Parliament was also uneasy with his declaration of the Divine Right of Kings.

His reign began deceptively calmly when James made peace with Spain in 1604. At home, he disappointed both Catholics and Puritans, who had hoped for more tolerance. The former suffered when a secret plan by a group of Catholics to blow up the King and parliament was uncovered and stopped, becoming known as the Gunpowder Plot. For their part, many Puritans left the country, including those who sailed in 1620 on board the *Mayflower* to seek freedom in America.

James' relationship with parliament also came apart. After lengthy arguments over control of finances, with parliament refusing to grant him more funds, the King dissolved the body in 1611. He called only two other parliaments into being and dissolved them both: one that sat for two months in 1614 and was nicknamed the Addled Parliament for accomplishing nothing; and one in 1621 to raise funds for his desire of an alliance with Spain, which was another failure.

James wrote several political treatises and poems and, more importantly, oversaw the publication in 1611 of a new English translation of the Bible, still known as the King James Version. He died in 1625 and was succeeded by his son, Charles.

The Gunpowder Plot

The plot in 1605 to rid the country of King James and destroy parliament during its ceremonial opening was devised by a handful of Catholics from the Midlands who were upset at the unexpected persecutions by the new King. They intended to blow up parliament at its opening session, kill the King and kidnap Prince Charles and Princess Elizabeth to begin a Catholic revolution. The leading plotter, Robert Catesby, gathered a small close group to agree the details. This plan was known by a few Catholic priests who attempted to

BELOW: The scheme to blow up parliament was well planned, but suffered from having too many plotters. They also failed by refusing to call off the plot after learning a government minister had been tipped off.

discourage them, but who did not inform the government. The plotters first rented a house next to the House of Lords in order to dig a tunnel beneath it and set off their explosives, but the task proved too difficult. They next rented a cellar underneath the Lords, and Guy Fawkes, using the name of John Johnson, set about storing 36 barrels of gunpowder under piles of coal and firewood. Parliament was set to open on 5 November 1605.

The plot began to unravel when an anonymous letter was received on 25 October by Lord Monteagle, a Catholic noble, warning him not to attend the opening because members 'shall receive a terrible blow this parliament and yet they shall not see who hurts them.' Monteagle passed the letter to Robert Cecil, the Earl of Salisbury and the King's key minister. One of Monteagle's servants, however, tipped off the conspirators who nevertheless decided to continue with their plan. On 4 November, the Privy Council had the cellar searched twice, first by the Earl of Suffolk and again during the evening by Thomas Knyvett, a Member of Parliament for Westminster, who was joined by a friend. They found the gunpowder being watched over by Fawkes and arrested him.

The next morning, learning that their scheme had been discovered, most of the conspirators fled to the Midlands, where they tried but failed to rally a Catholic force to overthrow the government. Authorities caught up with the leaders on the morning of 8 November at Holbeach House in Staffordshire. A

ABOVE: **Four leaders of the gunpowder plot were killed in a shootout. Guy Fawkes and the remaining conspirators were dragged on 31 January 1606 to the Old Palace Yard in Westminster where they were hanged, drawn and quartered.**

'They intended to kill the King and kidnap Prince Charles and Princess Elizabeth.'

BURNING OF THE GUY

Guy Fawkes was an experienced fighter, a powerful and intelligent man who had experience with gunpowder and seemed perfect to find, store, guard and detonate the explosives. When he was arrested and taken to the Tower, Fawkes endured several tortures, including the rack, but remained silent, a courage that impressed King James who said he had 'a Roman resolution.' After surviving two days of unbearable pain, Fawkes signed a confession and declared that the reason for so much gunpowder was 'to blow you Scotch beggars back to your native mountains.' As a traitor, he was sentenced to be hanged, drawn and quartered on 31 January 1606 in the Old Palace Yard of Westminster opposite parliament. Fawkes watched the three other conspirators undergo this horrible death, but then avoided it by leaping from the gallows and breaking his neck. The disappointed executioner had to hack apart the dead body so the quarters could be sent around the country as a warning.

Fawkes became a symbol of Catholic extremism and his effigy has been placed on bonfires lit each year on the 5th of November to celebrate the failed plot. The religious meaning of Guy Fawkes Night has virtually disappeared, and effigies of politicians and others sometimes replace the Guy, but the annual bonfires and fireworks continue along with the old rhyme that begins, 'Remember, remember, The fifth of November.' Guy Fawkes masks are also popular that day, and youths might still 'beg' strangers for 'A penny for the guy.'

BELOW: King James was impressed with Guy Fawkes' refusal to speak, but two days of intense torture eventually forced his confession.

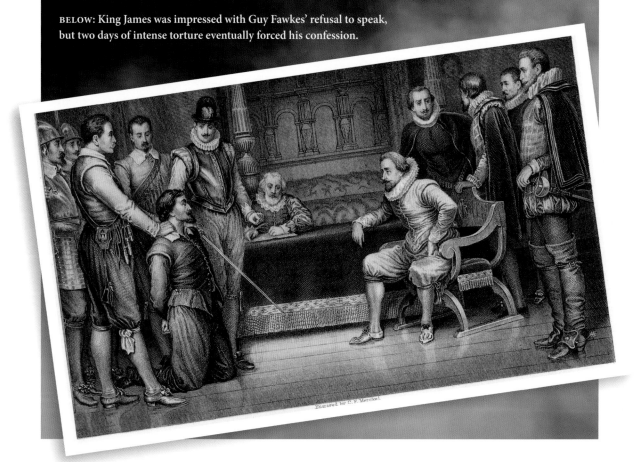

shootout killed Christopher and John (Jack) Wright, Robert Catesby and Thomas Percy. Two others, Thomas Winter and Ambrose Rookwood, were captured and taken back to London. All the conspirators were executed except Francis Tresham, who died in the Tower. He was the brother-in-law of Lord Monteagle and likely wrote the letter exposing the plot.

Today before the annual State Opening of Parliament, the cellars are traditionally searched by the Yeoman of the Guard to ensure that no conspirators and explosives are hidden there.

The Damned Crew

London's streets continued to be dangerous in the seventeenth century due to criminals who worked alone or in gangs. These could range from hoodlum robbers to gentlemen intent on mischievous mayhem. One of the earliest gangs of the latter was the Damned Crew. Usually drunk and rude, its members would look for fights, particularly with the evening watch.

One of their leaders in 1600 was Sir Edmund 'Pox' Baynham who had dropped his law studies in 1595 to become a roguish adventurer. On 18 March 1600, Baynham and other rowdies became drunk in the Mermaid Tavern on London's Cheapside and spilled onto the street looking for trouble. They marched loudly with their daggers and rapiers drawn until confronted by a watch who, with the help of others, fought the gang and overpowered them. They were taken to prison with Baynham yelling that he cared 'not a fart for the Lord Mayor or any magistrate in London.' On the urging of Queen Elizabeth, who was upset by their 'great and outrageous disorder,' they were specially tried at the Star Chamber court at Westminster Palace. They confessed and blamed their behaviour on 'drink and heat,' each receiving a £200 fine and a prison sentence.

Baynham then became captain of the Damned Crew and in 1603 was jailed for making 'some desperate speeches' against the new King, James I. He was later suspected of being linked to the Gunpowder Plot. During Guy Fawkes' trial, the attorney general called Baynham 'a fit messenger for the devil.' After this close call, he spent the remainder of his life roaming around Europe.

Death of an Adventurer

James I never liked Sir Walter Raleigh, the flamboyant explorer who flourished under Queen Elizabeth. His accomplishments were stunning: in 1578 he sailed to America and in 1584 and 1589 attempted unsuccessfully to establish the first English colony there (in present North Carolina), which he named Virginia in honour of his Virgin Queen. Credited with introducing the potato and tobacco to England, he became a favourite with Elizabeth, who knighted him in 1585, but when she learned of his secret marriage to one of her maids of honour, she threw both into the Tower in 1592. When he bought his release, Raleigh decided to win the Queen's heart back by a spectacular

'Fawkes endured several tortures, including the rack, but remained silent.'

BELOW: Sir Walter Raleigh placed Queen Elizabeth's standard in America to claim her territory. His heroic adventures and fame did not save him from the wrath of her successor, King James I, who had him executed.

expedition in 1595 to locate the fabled golden city of El Dorado in what is now Venezuela, but it was nowhere to be found.

When he became King in 1603, James accused Raleigh of plotting against him and returned him to the Tower under a death sentence. He reduced this to life, and Raleigh remained there for 12 years, taking advantage of the time to write the first volume of his *History of the World*. Released in 1616 without a pardon, he set off once more to find El Dorado. His forces burned a Spanish settlement in Guiana and Raleigh, suffering with fever, missed the action that killed his son, Walter. He again came home empty-handed and, much worse, had disobeyed the King's orders to maintain peace with the Spaniards.

James reinstated the death sentence at the request of Spain, and Raleigh was beheaded at the Tower on 29 October 1618. He made a short speech, saying his life had been 'a course of vanity.' He reminded the onlookers that he had been a seafaring man, a soldier and a courtier, before concluding with, 'I have a long journey to make and must bid the company farewell.' Before dying without a blindfold, he examined the axe himself and told the executioner, 'This is sharp medicine, but it is a physician for all diseases.'

'His skull was cracked and one eye dangled from its socket.'

A Witch in London?

Beliefs in witches, warlocks, wizards and magicians were prevalent in seventeenth century London. One man, John Lambe, had the misfortune to be called all four.

After first tutoring children, Lambe began to dabble in astrology and medicine, giving himself the title of doctor. He also told fortunes and claimed the ability to find lost items. In 1608, he was found guilty of sapping the strength of Lord Windsor and confessed that he had used a crystal ball to summon up four evil spirits. After the trial, several jurors died mysteriously, so Lambe's guilty verdict was suspended. He was finally locked up in 1622 for being close to spirits and was transferred the following year to the King's Bench Prison in London where influential people visited for his powders and potions, including George Villiers, the future Duke of Buckingham. When he was accused of raping an 11-year-old girl who delivered herbs to his two-room cell, Lambe was found guilty and sentenced to death, but pardoned by the crown. He became known as 'Buckingham's wizard,' giving his patron love charms to seduce women and credited with sending a mist over his house.

On 13 June 1628, Lambe, probably in his early 80s, went to see a play at the open-air Fortune Playhouse just outside the city. A group of young rowdies recognized him and when it ended they followed him home in the dark, howling and calling him a witch and devil. The hostile crowd grew and Lambe paid soldiers he passed to protect him. He sought refuge in a tavern, but was ejected because the owner feared the angry mob.

When his bodyguards left him as well, Lambe was jostled and pushed by his tormentors, who seemed unworried about his alleged mystical powers. They

John Lambe alias D.ʳLambe

From a rare Wood Cut in the Collection of Rob. Stearne Tighe Esq.

ABOVE: This woodcut captured John Lambe in all his finery. During one indictment, a witness accused Lambe of boasting he could 'intoxicate, poison and bewitch any man so as they should be disabled from begetting of children.'

attacked him near St Paul's Cathedral with stones and clubs so that his skull was cracked and one eye dangled from its socket. Lambe was reportedly carrying a crystal ball and several knives. Those in the crowd agreed that justice had finally been done, and none of them were ever arrested.

That same year saw a ballad, 'The Tragedy of Doctor Lambe' and a pamphlet, 'A briefe description of the notorious life of John Lambe.' In 1634, a play entitled 'Doctor Lambe and the Witches' was produced.

Beheading a King

Charles I was born in 1600, the son of James I and Anne of Denmark. He married Henrietta Maria, the Catholic daughter of Henry IV of France, which introduced Catholics into the English court. After taking the throne in 1625, Charles repeated the major mistake of his father by constantly battling with parliament. Their dispute centred on the King's desire to raise revenues by taxation. He called and dissolved three parliaments before deciding to rule by himself in 1629 and did so for 11 years. When tensions increased between Catholics and Puritans, his restrictions drove many members of both from England. When Charles attempted to force a new prayer book on the Scots, they rebelled. Needing funds for that battle, the King again convened parliament in 1640, but it was dissolved less than a month later and is now known as the 'Short Parliament.' The 'Long Parliament' in 1642 fared worse when Charles tried to arrest five members of the House of Commons, but they had already fled.

BELOW: The Battle of Naseby south of Leicester saw Oliver Cromwell's New Model Army of 14,000 win a decisive victory over the royalist army of nearly 10,000. Cromwell took some 4000 prisoners and virtually ended the war.

The execution of Charles I took place on 30 January 1649 outside the Banqueting House of Whitehall Palace. Iron staples were attached to the floor in case the King needed to be forcibly restrained with ropes.

That same year, civil war broke out, with the King's troops (the Cavaliers) facing parliament's forces (the Roundheads). Oliver Cromwell, the Puritan leader of parliament's New Model Army, routed Charles' army on 14 June 1645 at the Battle of Naseby and continued to be victorious. The next year, the King surrendered to Scottish troops, and in 1646 they handed him over to parliament. He was imprisoned on the Isle of Wight, but escaped in 1647 to rally dissident Scots to his cause and to another defeat by Cromwell. Tried for treason, Charles refused to enter a plea arguing that the court was not legitimate. He was found guilty by a vote of 68 to 67.

'No mercy was shown as Cromwell's force slaughtered some 2500 men.'

His public execution on 30 January 1649 was a beheading in London on a scaffold outside the Banqueting House of Whitehall Palace. He made his way there through a removed upstairs window. Black drapes hid the scene from most of the crowd, but some watched from rooftops. The day was especially cold, and the King wore two shirts so he would not shiver as if afraid. He made a speech, declaring himself 'a martyr of the people' and told the Bishop of London, 'I go from a corruptible crown to an incorruptible crown where no disturbance can be.' He asked the executioner if his hair troubled him and was given help to tuck it under his cap. He also requested that the block be made level. Told that it was, he suggested it should be slightly higher, but was informed that this was not possible. The King placed his head on it, stretched out his hands and was beheaded with one blow.

BELOW: Oliver Cromwell had a forceful character and was a fiery, outspoken speaker. Deeply religious, he believed he was one of God's Chosen, though he once said he had been 'the chief of sinners' in his youth.

The Lord Protector

Having defeated the Royal army and overseen the execution of a King, Oliver Cromwell became the most powerful man in England and used that power as a dictator. Like the Kings before him, he argued constantly with parliament and dissolved it.

Cromwell came from a wealthy family in Huntingdonshire. He studied for a while at Cambridge and became a Member of Parliament, and was known for his extreme Puritan views and commanding voice. He was one of the leaders who opposed the King's request to raise taxes and demanded that Charles yield more power to parliament. When the civil war broke out, Cromwell organized a disciplined, loyal New Model Army and inflicted defeats on the Royal forces, including their allies in Scotland.

With the return of peace, Cromwell had his army forcibly remove 110 members of the 'Long Parliament,' reducing it to a 'Rump' one in 1648. He removed the rest in 1653 at the point of swords and replaced it with a parliament of 'Puritan Saints' chosen by himself. It was known as the Barebones Parliament, because one member, Praisegod Barebone, was amazingly a Baptist. When it proved just as unable to govern, Cromwell dissolved it in 1655 and ruled alone as Lord Protector of the Commonwealth until his death in 1658. His son, Richard, was named his successor, but his weak rule and the public's dislike for strict Puritan values and cuts to the army led to the restoration of the monarchy two years later.

A Slaughter in Ireland

When Catholics in Ireland resisted English rule and seemed a danger to Cromwell, his New Model Army invaded in 1649 and overwhelmed the fortified town of Drogheda on Ireland's east coast. No mercy was shown as Cromwell's force slaughtered some 2500 men, mostly soldiers, but including Catholic priests, many being clubbed to death. From there, the army attacked Wexford with equal brutality, saying this was 'the judgment of God' and revenge for the past massacre of Protestants. This allowed the confiscation of lands belonging to native Catholics and their redistribution to Protestants from England, which involved nearly 40 per cent of all Ireland.

BELOW: The massacre at Drogheda by Cromwell's forces was especially brutal. One officer recalled trying to save a beautiful woman who knelt pleading, but another soldier stabbed her with his sword and she was thrown onto rocks.

Cromwell came back to London the following year, 1650, and turned his attention to the Scots who had proclaimed Charles II as King. Charles marched his force south, meeting Cromwell's army at Worcester where he was soundly defeated. Charles escaped and his supporters were suppressed with less brutality than had befallen the Irish. An English occupational force was established in the Scottish Lowlands until, ironically, Charles was restored to the English throne in 1660. As King, he quickly ordered that Cromwell's body be exhumed and put on trial. It was found guilty, hanged on the Tyburn gallows and the head put on display.

RIGHT: Charles II took revenge on Cromwell's body, which was dug up in Westminster Abbey and hung, then beheaded. The head was impaled on a spike and placed on the roof of Westminster Hall, remaining there for 25 years.

The Restoration

When his father was beheaded, Charles II escaped to France and then Holland before returning to Scotland to accept its kingship. After the 1651 defeat of his army of 10,000 men by Cromwell, the English placed a bounty of £1000 on his head. He avoided capture for six weeks before fleeing again to France and Europe for eight years. When the Protectorate failed, he was asked to return to restore the monarchy and finally put an end to the strict Puritan prohibitions. His triumphant march into London on 29 May 1660, his 30th birthday, was met with rejoicing and thanksgiving among the 500,000 population. Good feelings abounded and the King withheld retribution to most of the 20 or so still living who had signed his father's death warrant, although nine were executed. The Earl of Clarendon urged the new parliament to restore 'the whole nation to its primitive temper and integrity, to its good old manners, its good old humour and its good old nature.'

AN END TO JOY

Life under the Puritan rule of Cromwell was trying for Londoners as they saw their pleasures disappear one by one. The theatres and inns were closed and bans enforced on sports, such as horseracing, bearbaiting and even football. Penalties, including the stocks, were enforced on a Sunday as a religious day. This forbade most types of work, travel and the pointless enjoyment of a Sunday walk (unless to church). Profanity at any time led to fines or even prison. Black clothes were required, so colourful dresses were deemed a sin. Enforcers would also stop a woman in the streets to rub off any makeup. Even Christmas was to be strictly religious with no celebrations, carols, decorations or such joys as turkey, mince pies and ale.

LEFT: **Charles II was welcomed with joy as he rode through London. Seeing the happiness, he joked that it was his fault to stay away so long, since everyone he met said they had always wished that he would return.**

Charles' reign saw the monarch's turning point with parliament that now took the upper hand with political parties formed for the first time: Cavaliers became the Tory Party supporting the King's supremacy, while Roundheads created the Whig Party backing parliament's power. Whigs also stirred up anti-Catholic feelings to block the King's Catholic brother, James, from succeeding him.

Charles' rule was riddled with financial problems and a weak defence and foreign policy. One dispute with Holland brought a Dutch fleet up the River Medway near London to burn five battleships and tow the 80-gun first-rate

Londoners were terrified in June 1667 when the Dutch fleet sailed up the Medway past poor river defences to within 48km (30 miles) of the city. The invaders burned or sank five large English ships at their moorings.

three-decker *Royal Charles* back to Holland. At the same time, Charles had the misfortune to reign during two disasters, the Great Plague of 1665 and the Great Fire in 1666.

These tragedies did not dampen the King's love for an easy and pleasurable life. In 1662, he married Catherine of Braganza, and his Portuguese bride brought along a dowry of about £300,000. His love life also revolved around a line of 13 known mistresses, including the renowned Nell Gwyn, with perhaps others unknown.

Pretty, Witty Nell

The actress Nell Gwyn, born Eleanor Gwynne in Hereford, was Charles most beloved mistress. Raised in her mother's 'bawdyhouse' near Covent Garden, she had already been the mistress of an actor and the Earl of Dorset before the King took over in 1669. She cheekily called him Charles III, because her first two lovers were also named Charles. Once when mistaken for a lady in her carriage, she said, 'Pray, good people, be civil, I am the Protestant whore.' An excellent singer and dancer, she was a star of the King's Company, especially in comedy roles, and was known for her wit, joyful nature and indiscretions. The diarist Samuel Pepys called her 'pretty, witty Nell.' She also had a wicked sense of humour. Learning in 1668 that the King intended to sleep with another mistress, Moll Davis, also a comic actress, Nell gave the woman sweetmeats laced with a laxative. The evening of love went poorly, and Charles broke off relations with Moll.

Nell and Charles had sons in 1670 and 1671. Given an expensive London home and taken to the Royal court, Nell remained the King's love for the rest of his life. On his deathbed in 1685, knowing she had massive debts, Charles instructed his brother, the future King, 'Let not poor Nelly starve.' James II honoured the request, paying off Nell's debts and providing an annual pension of £1500 until her death in 1687.

The King's Wild Mistress

Charles II's many mistresses waged a fierce competition among themselves, but one was bold enough to battle the King himself. Barbara Palmer, born Barbara Villiers, was beautiful, a tall and auburn-haired married woman who gave birth to a daughter, Anne, in 1661 a few months after the arrival of Charles' new bride from Portugal, Catherine of Braganza. Charles was suspicious about who was the father, but he continued to visit his mistress four nights a week at her home in Whitehall. She became the Countess of Castlemaine in 1661 and the following year had a son, but the King denied paternity. When he brought his mistress to Catherine that year as her new Lady of the Bedchamber, the Queen fainted and bled from the nose. Charles would have wild arguments with Barbara who issued various threats. A bishop had once described her as 'enormously vicious and ravenous.' When she was expecting again in 1667, she promised she would

ABOVE: Nell Gwyn would never have performed or flourished under Cromwell's Puritan rule, but her heart-shaped face, shapely figure and joy for life made her an apt symbol for the high spirits of the Restoration.

dash the child's brains out in front of Charles if he denied paternity. He refused, but returned in a few days to apologize. In 1670, she became the Countess of Southampton and Duchess of Cleveland. Eventually, her furious temper and other affairs were too much to take, and Charles turned to other mistresses in 1674, especially Louise, the Duchess of Portsmouth. Barbara moved to Paris in 1677 for four years, having more affairs before returning to have a nostalgic but not close friendship with the King just before his death in 1685. He was possibly the father of several of her seven children.

> ## 'She promised she would dash the child's brains out in front of Charles.'

Quaker Persecution

The Quaker movement, viewed with suspicion by Puritans, had adopted its name from a judge's description after one of its leaders, George Fox 'bade them tremble at the word of the Lord.' This happened during Fox's trial in 1650, and he would go on to be imprisoned eight times between 1649 and 1673. Quakers believed in a direct relationship to God without the formal trappings of a church and priest. They refused to attend church, take oaths, pay tithes, be baptized with water or engage in any other association with organized religion. By 1657, between 700 and 1000 Quakers were held in prison.

After the Restoration, harsher penalties were introduced to suppress the Quakers and other Separatist movements. In 1662, two years after Charles II became King, parliament passed the Act of Uniformity requiring strict adherence to worship in the Church of England. Fox continued to be arrested and Quaker meetings became illegal because of a law banning meetings of more than five people.

Persecution of Quakers officially ended under the next monarch, James II, with passage of the Toleration Act in 1689.

LEFT: George Fox, shown here in prison, travelled to North America to organize Quaker communities in Maryland and Rhode Island. George Fox University in Oregon was named for him and today has more than 4000 students.

ABOVE: Torture and public humiliation were imposed on James Naylor, who barely escaped being executed. He renounced his possessions and was an excellent preacher whose enthusiasm and charisma won many converts during his street appeals.

The Torturing of James Naylor

A renowned Quaker preacher in London by 1655, James Naylor was imprisoned the next year and had a subsequent falling out with George Fox, the competing leader of the movement, after Fox visited him in prison and Naylor refused to kiss his hand. Naylor was released, but again arrested for riding Christ-like into Bristol on 20 October 1656 while his followers sang and cast garments before him. Their group was arrested and charged with blasphemy. Naylor survived a vote in the House of Commons to execute him, with some members urging he be stoned to death under Old Testament law.

Although Oliver Cromwell called for leniency, Naylor's punishment turned out to be severe. He was put in a pillory, whipped through London and Bristol where he was forced to repeat his ride sitting backwards on his horse. He also had his forehead branded with the letter 'B' for blasphemer, a hot iron was bored through his tongue and he was forced to do hard labour. Released in 1659 after the 'Rump Parliament' declared an amnesty for Quakers, he began preaching again in London where he met Fox and made amends. In October 1660, thieves attacked him on his way home to Yorkshire and he died the next day in a local Quaker's home.

OPPOSITE: Slave ships were torture in themselves, with slaves kept in tiny spaces below decks in leg shackles, handcuffs and chains. Minimum amounts of food and water were allowed, and some deaths were normal during a voyage.

Slavery and London

In 1660, Charles II granted a charter to the Royal Adventurers into Africa that began seizing and transporting slaves as well as goods such as gold. The company shipped thousands of slaves to the West Indies, earning about £100,000 in 1665. Investors included members of the Royal family and the diarist Samuel Pepys. This was an expansion of the slave trade approved by Charles I, who had licensed companies in that brutal business. The trade had existed under Elizabeth I, who naively wanted assurances that no person would be enslaved without their consent, which slave traders assured her had been given.

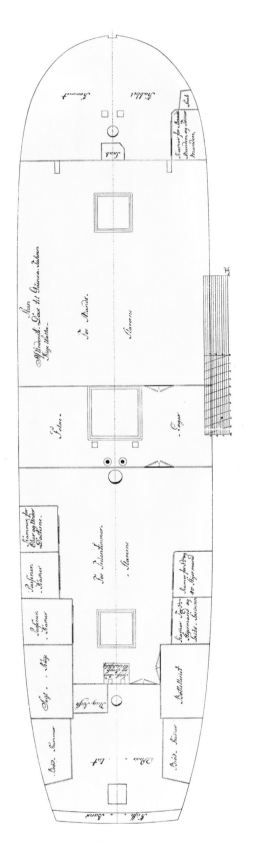

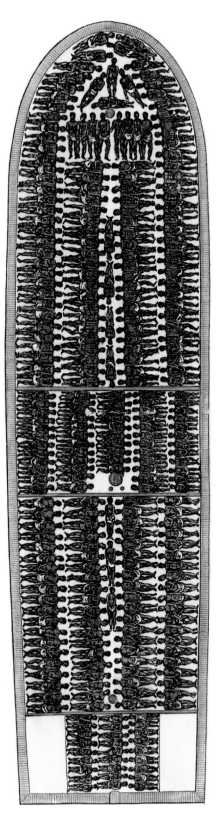

By the seventeenth century, colonies were being established in America and the demand for West African slaves was increasing. In 1672, the Royal Adventurers enterprise collapsed, but that same year another, the Royal African Company, was established, governed by the Duke of York. It transported some 90,000 slaves to America between 1672 and 1689 to work on cotton, tobacco and sugar plantations. It was 'fashionable' in the late seventeenth century for a Londoner to own a slave. Some did escape and were hidden in safe houses while their owners posted rewards for their 'lost property.'

The slave trade, which had been financed by the city's financial institutions, would not be abolished until 1807, with Londoners leading the way by sending petitions to parliament and boycotting products made by slave labour. It is believed that more than 450,000 slaves died on British ships during their terrible passages to America.

'40,000 dogs and 200,000 cats were killed as possible carriers of the disease.'

The Great Plague

Other plague epidemics had struck London, but the Great Plague of 1665 swept through the city's growing population of some 460,000 and officially killed 68,596, although the number was possibly as high as 100,000. The first deaths occurred in April and by September about 7000 were dying each week, being collected in carts for mass burials in large pits at Southwark and Cripplegate. Those who transported the dead were prohibited from mixing with the general population.

Theatres, inns and other public places were closed. Infected houses were quarantined and marked with a red 'X,' with 'God have mercy upon us' often written across the door, because many felt the plague was a judgment of God. Residents burned rotting rubbish and tried more extreme measures: an estimated 40,000 dogs and 200,000 cats were killed as possible carriers of the disease. Virtually nothing could be done to save victims, although a few did survive. Doctors would bleed the tell-tale spots on the skin, but this only weakened their patients.

The best defence was to leave the city, as did Charles and his court, moving in July to Hampton Court and then further to Oxford, where parliament met in October. Those Londoners who could afford it also stayed in the countryside

TOO FANCY DRESS

When the Puritan government ended, so did its restrictions on dress. The reaction was a joyful flamboyance in clothes and fashion that included the feminine look for wealthy men. They began wearing short breeches whose width made them resemble petticoats. Colourful ribbons fluttered from their perfumed clothes and bright stockings. Their heads were topped by feathered hats and elaborate curly periwigs that fell below the shoulders. The well-dressed gentleman might also carry a muff and apply cosmetics and a patch on his face. The general public was amused, and diarist Samuel Pepys recounted his friend mistakenly putting both legs together in one leg of his breeches and going out and about that way. For his part, the King was not amused, complaining to parliament about the excess of the feminine clothes.

DIARY OF THE PLAGUE

Samuel Pepys made detailed observations of the plague that were recorded in his contemporary diary. Some of these in 1665 include:

August 28th – But now, how few people I see, and those walking like people that have taken leave of the world.

August 31st – Every day sadder and sadder news of its increase. In the City died this week 7496; and of them, 6102 of the plague. But it is feared that the true number of the dead this week is near 10,000 – partly from the poor that cannot be taken notice of through the greatness of the number, and partly from the Quakers and others that will not have any bell ring for them.

September 14th – …my meeting dead corps's of the plague, carried to be buried close to me at noonday through the City in Fanchurch-street – to see a person sick of the sores carried close to me by Grace-church in a hackney-coach – my finding the Angell tavern at the lower end of Tower-hill shut up; and more than that, the alehouse at the Tower-stairs; and more than that, that the person was then dying of the plague when I was last there…

December 31st – Yet to our great joy, the town fills apace, and shops begin to open again. Pray God continue the plague's decrease – for that keeps the Court away from the place of business, and so all goes to wrack as to public matters, they at this distance not thinking of it.

during the summer, some taking the plague with them, but the poor had no escape from their rat-infested streets and no money for special treatments.

The plague diminished that winter and died away during the Great Fire in September 1666. Other cities also suffered, from Newcastle to Southampton, with England losing an estimated three-quarters of a million lives.

The Great Fire

London's Great Fire began on 2 September 1666 and lasted four days. It burned down 13,200 houses, 87 parish churches, St Paul's Cathedral built in the Middle Ages, the Royal Exchange and the Guildhall. The flames spread so quickly because the city had experienced a summer drought and its tightly packed houses were built of timber covered in pitch.

'Losses were estimated at £10 million, with many people ruined financially.'

The fire began in Thomas Farynor's bakery in Pudding Lane. He thought he had extinguished it in the oven, but embers flared up three hours later at 1 a.m. He, his wife, daughter and a servant escaped through an upstairs window, but a maid died, the fire's first victim.

A strong wind carried the inferno down to the Thames where warehouses were stocked with oil and other flammable materials. The city still had no fire brigade, so residents fought a losing battle using basics like leather water buckets and axes. They carried as many valuables as they could to the river, trying to escape on boats and barges, or fled to outlying fields to live in tents. The government ordered burning houses to be pulled down, but this had little effect on the spreading fire. Even the King was seen fighting the flames. The diarist Samuel Pepys was clerk to the Royal Navy and agreed with the admiral that houses should be blown up to stop the fire's advance. This was done with gunpowder, and the fire was stopped the next morning, 5 September.

Losses were estimated at £10 million, with many people ruined financially. Only 16 people were verified as being killed by the fire, which did have positive outcomes: the Great Plague was eradicated, fire brigades established, many streets widened and much of London rebuilt with brick and stone, often with spectacular results such as Sir Christopher Wren's St Paul's Cathedral. The fire had destroyed 87 churches, and Wren also oversaw the building of 52 new ones.

A 61m (202ft) monument remembering the fire was completed in 1677 near the site where it started.

DIARY OF THE FIRE

Samuel Pepys' diary recounted the Great Fire that he witnessed and fought. The entry for Sunday, 2 September 1666, includes:

Everybody endeavouring to remove their goods, and flinging into the river or bringing them into lighters [barges] that layoff; poor people staying in their houses as long as till the very fire touched them, and then running into boats, or clambering from one pair of stairs by the water-side to another… every creature coming away loaden with goods to save, and here and there sicke people carried away in beds. Extraordinary good goods carried in carts and on backs… So near the fire as we could for smoke; and all over the Thames, with one's face in the wind, you were almost burned with a shower of firedrops. This is very true; so as houses were burned by these drops and flakes of fire, three or four, nay, five or six houses, one from another… it was dark almost, and saw the fire grow; and, as it grew darker, appeared more and more, and in corners and in steeples, and between churches and houses, as far as we could see up the hill to the City, in a most horrid, malicious bloody flame, not like the fine flame of an ordinary fire… it made me weep to see it. The Churches, houses and all on fire and flaming at once; and the horrid noise the flames made, and the cracking of houses at their ruins.

RIGHT: Samuel Pepys began his diary, which was written in shorthand, in 1660 when he was 27 and wrote it until 1669.

The Great Fire destroyed five-sixths of the medieval walled city with no buildings escaping some damage. London Bridge, however, survived. For days smoke continued to rise and the ground remained too hot to walk upon.

The Popish Plot

In 1678, London and the country were gripped by a false story of a Jesuit plan to assassinate Charles II so his Catholic brother, the Duke of York (later James I) could take the throne. The rumour was fabricated by Titus Oates, a Church of England priest, who in 1677 became a Catholic. In September 1678, he swore before a justice of the peace, Sir Edmund Berry Godfrey, that the plot was true, and when Sir Edmund was murdered in October Londoners were gripped by panic. Oates was brought before the Privy Council where Charles himself questioned him and was unconvinced. Nevertheless, the city hailed him as a hero.

The frenzy caused by his story led to about 35 people being executed and others dying in prison. Two innocent victims of the Popish Plot were the Jesuits William Ireland and John Gove. Oates himself led constables to arrest Ireland and testified against him. Ireland had an alibi backed by witnesses that the King believed, but the judges did not. Their verdict of guilty in 1678 at London's Old Bailey said the two men had contrived a 'Hellish Plot' and they failed to show 'any respect either for their King, Countrey or Religion; or indeed for themselves, their

RIGHT: Titus Oates is depicted in the pillory and surrounded by innocent victims (with knives in their hearts) whom he identified as part of the Popish Plot. Two wrongly accused were executed, but Oates survived and was pardoned.

Estates, lives, wives or children.' The two were taken together to Tyburn to be hanged, drawn and quartered for high treason, but the still doubting King ordered they should be dead from the hanging to spare them extra pain.

Eventually evidence was found that indicated the plot had been fabricated. The Duke of York sued Oates and was awarded £100,000. He became King in 1685, and Oates was convicted of perjury and imprisoned until 1688 when William of Orange deposed James. Strangely, Oates then became a Baptist in 1693.

'He lacked experience of beheadings and became notorious for his sloppy work.'

The Bloody Assizes

James II hardly had a honeymoon period after he succeeded his brother, Charles II, in 1685. Within six months, the Duke of Monmouth, James Scott, was challenging the King, his uncle, who had converted to Catholicism in 1669. Monmouth was the illegitimate son of Charles II and a Protestant who won enthusiastic support when he landed at Lyme Regis, Dorset, and raised 4000 men, mostly peasants. Enthusiasm was not enough, however, when his army, some wielding pitchforks, faced the King's forces on the plain of Sedgemoor, Somerset, on 6 July 1685 and was routed. Monmouth fled in a shepherd's disguise, but was captured and beheaded on Tower Hill on 15 July by the fumbling axeman, Jack Ketch, who took at least five blows to dispatch him.

This rebellion was followed by the 'Bloody Assizes' of Judge George Jeffreys, the infamous Lord Chief Justice known for his cruelty and corruption. The trials with four other judges resulted in the hanging of about 320 who had supported Monmouth. Several hundreds died in prison, others were flogged or fined and more than 800 were transported from England to exile as virtual slaves in Barbados and other colonies.

For his part, James asked parliament to recognize the equality of both religions. This was part of his play to turn England back to Catholicism. When it refused, he suspended the body in 1685 and issued a Declaration of Indulgence for religious tolerance in 1687. This came too late. The following year, William of Orange, a leading Protestant in Europe, invaded and took the crown when James fled. Judge Jeffreys also attempted to flee disguised as a sailor, but was captured and sent to the Tower where he died four months later.

Jack Ketch

Jack Ketch, sometimes called John, was London's executioner from 1666 to 1678. He had a dislikeable personality and often showed up drunk to dispatch his victims. He was estimated to have killed hundreds, nearly all by hanging. For this reason, he lacked experience of beheadings and became notorious for his sloppy work, especially in his later years when he was employed occasionally. Two of his bungled jobs involved the convicted traitors William, Lord Russell and James, the Duke of Monmouth.

Ketch beheaded Lord Russell in 1683 during the late reign of Charles II after being found guilty of supporting a plot to kill the King. The executioner was given

ABOVE: George Jeffreys, a Welsh judge, was known as 'the hanging judge' because of his harsh sentences, especially seen in the Bloody Assizes after he bullied the defendants. He also extorted money from his victims.

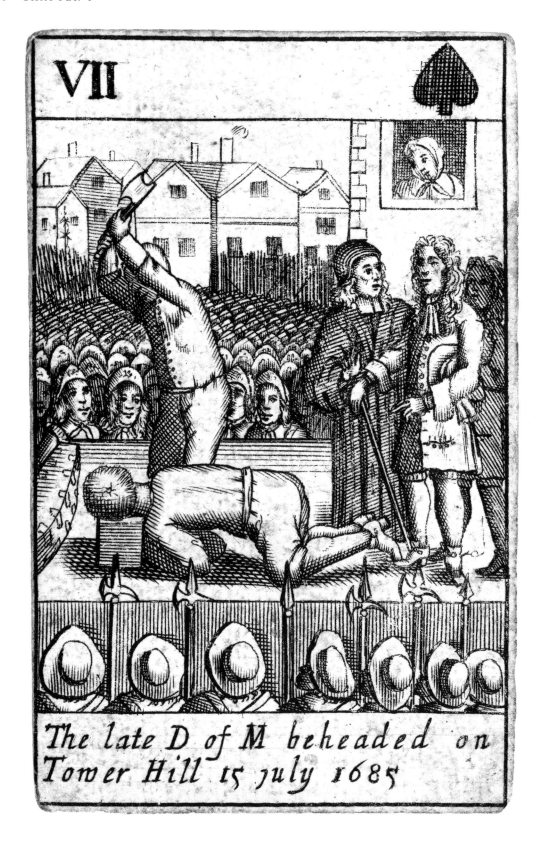

10 or more guineas to do a swift job, but took some five clumsy blows to remove Russell's head. Ketch received so much criticism he issued a written apology, but still blamed his victim for assuming the 'wrong posture' and failing to give the usual hand signal that he was ready.

Before Monmouth put his head on the block in 1685, he gave Ketch six guineas and told him 'do not hack me' as he had Lord Russell, adding, 'I have heard you struck him four or five times.' These words visibly increased Ketch's nervousness, and his first blow made only a slight wound, causing the victim to look back reproachfully at the axeman. After two more non-fatal attempts, Ketch threw down the axe and said, 'I cannot do it. My heart fails me.' Implored by the sheriff and crowd, he retrieved the axe and ended Monmouth's life with two more blows and then had to separate the head from the body with a knife. One onlooker later wrote that the angry crowd might have torn Ketch to pieces if he had not been protected by guards.

Ketch, who died a year after beheading Monmouth, was variously called incompetent or a butcher, and there were suspicions that authorities had requested the torturous executions. His name was used by parents to frighten children who misbehaved and later became the general name for any executioner.

'Then he had to separate the head from the body with a knife.'

The Midwife Who Murdered

Historians obviously concentrate on crimes committed by and on Royalty and other leaders, but common Londoners did more damage to one another, including gruesome murders. A case in point was the French midwife, Mary Awbry. She was a Huguenot, Mary Des Ormeaux, who married an English Catholic, Denis Awbry, who began to physically abuse her. Four years later in 1688 the violence became worse, and she plotted to murder him, even telling friends, 'I must kill him.'

The opportunity came on the dark morning of 27 January when he returned home drunk at 5 a.m, raped her and fell asleep. Mary strangled him, dismembered his body and, with the help of her son, John, from a previous marriage, hid the parts in several different places: his mangled torso was found on 31 January on a dunghill in Holborn and his arms and legs turned up in a sewer. Being the only obvious suspect, Mary was arrested and tried at the Old Bailey where she pleaded guilty. She was sentenced to be burned at the stake, which was carried out on 2 March in Leicester Fields (now Leicester Square).

Tragedy Off the Stage

A frequent type of murder in seventeenth-century London involved crimes of passion, and the perpetrators were often found innocent. A famous case on a street in London's theatre district involved the planned kidnapping of an actress, Anne Bracegirdle. She was beloved by audiences and by the 1690s was well known for her Shakespearean roles, including Desdemona in *Othello*.

BELOW: Anne Bracegirdle had a range of talents, acting in Shakespeare's plays and singing in light dramas. She retired when a younger actress, Anne Oldfield, became more popular. Bracegirdle is buried in the cloisters of Westminster Abbey.

Captain Richard Hill became infatuated with the actress and spent much time and attention pursuing her. Finally, he solicited the help of Charles, Baron Mohun, and a street gang of thugs to abduct Anne on 9 December 1692. She was to be held out of town for a week so that Hill could persuade her to marry him. The two men hired a coach for the kidnapping, equipped inside with several pistols and a change of clothes for Anne.

The kidnapping was foiled by the intervention of Anne's mother and neighbours. This turned Hill's attention to the actress' suspected lover, the actor William Mountford, whom he and Mohun ambushed that evening on Howard Street in the Strand. While Mohun looked on or perhaps restrained the victim, Hill stabbed the actor in the chest. He died the next day, and the murderer fled to France, leaving Mohun to face justice. After a five-day trial, the Baron's peers (friends in high places) found him innocent by a vote of 69 to 14.

Their intended victim, Anne, went on to become more famous on the stage. Hill later won a pardon for foreign service with the army, but supposedly died in a drunken tavern brawl. In 1697, Mohun killed a man in a duel and was again acquitted. In 1712, he fought a duel in Hyde Park with the Duke of Hamilton. Both died, but it was believed Mohun was shot dead and his second then killed Hamilton.

The Glorious Revolution

James II was ironically deposed by his daughter, Mary, and her husband who was his nephew, William, the Protestant Prince of Orange and Stadholder of the Netherlands. James' attempt to turn England into a Catholic country distressed most of his subjects, and on 10 June 1688 the birth of a son who would probably continue this policy led prominent politicians to write to William urging him to invade and take the throne. He accepted and landed in Devon on 5 November, gathering support as he advanced with his army towards London. Even James' own daughter, Princess Anne, deserted to William. Some resistance did occur, with 50 killed in Reading.

In London, rioting against Catholics broke out, and James fled to Kent on 11 December where he was captured by fishermen. Eager to see the last of him, William made arrangements and James was allowed to leave for France on 23 December.

Parliament had hoped Mary would rightfully rule with William as her consort, but she refused unless they ruled as William III and Mary II. In 1689, the King pushed through the Toleration Act protecting many Protestant groups, but not Catholics, and he agreed to parliament's Declaration of Rights that gave freedoms to that body, ending the crown's divine sovereignty.

> # 'Two men hired a coach for the kidnapping, equipped inside with several pistols.'

LEFT: James made a humiliating departure from his kingdom, being captured in Kent trying to flee to France. William had no desire to imprison him as a martyr and ordered that he be allowed to leave.

WILLIAM AND MARY AND ELIZABETH

William was one of the last Kings you would expect to have a mistress, but he conducted a discreet affair. When his marriage had been arranged to Mary, she reportedly found him ugly and cried day and night. Their relationship, however, became agreeable and then happy. William was not a candid man and remained careful about his interest in Elizabeth Villiers, one of Mary's ladies-in-waiting. She was the cousin of Barbara Villiers, who had been the mistress of Charles II. Although smart and witty, Elizabeth lacked Barbara's beauty and was even known as 'Squinting Betty' because of an eye problem. Also unlike her cousin, she was discreet.

Mary died in 1694, and the grieving King was pleased the next year when Elizabeth married a general of the Royal Scots. She remained a close, loyal friend of William and a fixture of the court. When he died in 1702, she hosted both George I and George II at her country estate before her death in 1733.

5

EIGHTEENTH CENTURY

Lo... of consumption and enjoyment
des...and the South Sea Bubble financial
cras...ued and many families lost sons
fight...

C HANG...hteenth century as the
city ad...More problems with
parlian...Tower. Many citizens
were achieving...widespread bread riots
and social unres...

Divided Londo
Londoners were str...r new and already
crowned Hanover K...sion through
the city in 1715. He su...reign, who
had taken the throne b...Parliament
excluded the deposed C...ting instead
the thin line through Jan...George of
the House of Hanover. Ge...English

OPPOSITE: As the century
turned, Londoners were
still basking in the afterglow
of the Restoration and the
Glorious Revolution. Times
seemed right to increase
both business and leisure,
but serious financial and
social problems awaited.

RIGHT: George I, the first Hanoverian King, only spoke German and had to communicate with his ministers in French. He was generally unpopular, as were his two mistresses, and rumours abounded about him mistreating his wife.

and he was never beloved by Londoners.

The population had reached some 630,000 by this time, and it was deeply split in economic terms. The favoured class would bring about many modern features for their city, from political coffee houses to a variety of newspapers, novels and Samuel Johnson's dictionary. Most Londoners existed in a state of poverty, still living in virtual medieval conditions with medieval mentalities.

Vicious crimes abounded and were described in a popular publication, *The Proceedings of the Old Bailey*, which tended to create anxiety among its readers, who worried about their city's social unrest.

GEORGE'S TWO MISTRESSES

England's new Hanoverian King arrived in 1715 with two mistresses among his entourage. He had already spent many years with them, and in 1694 his bored wife had had an affair with a Swedish count. George had her imprisoned in the Castle of Ahlden for the remaining 30 years of her life without ever seeing her two children again. George supposedly had two men kill the count and dump his body in a river.

Both mistresses were considered to be unattractive. One was so skinny, Londoners nicknamed her the 'Maypole', and the other so short and fat she was called the 'Elephant and Castle', a well-known London location. His 'Maypole' was Ehrengard Melusine von der Schulenburg, and they had three daughters. When he died in 1727, she lived with a pet raven that she believed to be the King's soul. His 'Elephant' was Sophia von Kielmansegg, who was his illegitimate half-sister.

RIGHT: Ehrengard, the 'Maypole', was George's favourite mistress. Among her several titles were Duchess of Kendall and Baroness of Glastonbury.

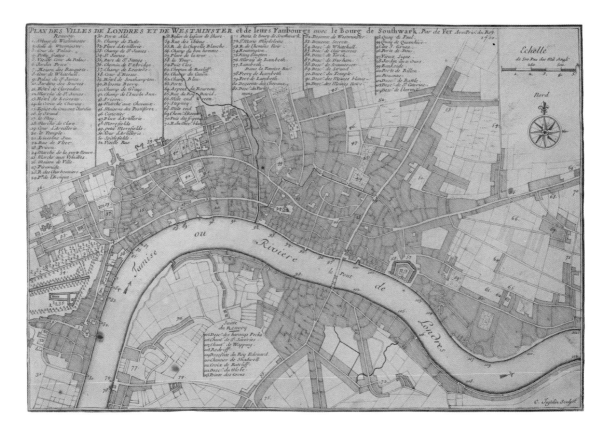

The Mug-house Riots

London rowdies often came together in gangs that were known as 'mobbers.' When George I became King he was supported by gentlemen – lawyers and statesmen who congregated in mug-houses, establishments for political groups and meetings. Several battles occurred in 1715 between mug-house members supporting the new King and street demonstrators, especially Jacobites calling for the return of James II to the throne.

On 23 July 1716, Whig loyalists in a mug-house in Salisbury Court, Fleet Street, began drinking to the health of the new King, calling out 'King George forever.' This irritated people on the street, who threw stones at people who entered the establishment while a constable on his station did nothing. The next morning a larger crowd gathered and threw stones at the pub, breaking most of its windows and threatening to pull the building down for a bonfire on Fleet Street. A constable read a proclamation ordering them to disperse, but this made things worse. Cries went up among the mob of 'No King George. No Hanoverians. Down with the mug-house.' One man brought three bottles out of the pub and drank to the health of the Stuart pretender, James. Some men inside went out to drive the attackers down Fleet Street, but were overwhelmed and took shelter on the upper floor of the pub while the rioters trashed the downstairs, throwing items out onto the courtyard for the mobbers to destroy. A defender was pushed into the courtyard and beaten with sticks and clubs.

ABOVE: London's population had grown by about one million by the end of the eighteenth century. The first signs of an industrial revolution were evident, and London was becoming the centre of the great British Empire.

'London rowdies often came together in gangs that were know as "mobbers."'

About 11 a.m., one customer, supposedly Robert Read, fired at the rioters with a blunderbuss musket and killed Daniel Vaughan, known as Vinegar. A trial was held on 6 September before a grand jury, and the accused was acquitted of murder. Five mobbers, however, were found guilty of riot and rebellion and executed at Tyburn.

The Hellfire Club

The original Hellfire Club was founded in 1719 in London by a duke, Philip Warton, and some of his friends. Its purpose was to enliven normally dull Sundays by coming together to drink, sing bawdy songs and satirize the Catholic religion and its rituals. The club was closed down two years later by Royal edict because, among other things, it encouraged members to 'corrupt the minds and morals of one another.'

The better remembered Hellfire Club was established in 1746 by the infamous Sir Francis Dashwood, former Chancellor of the Exchequer, under the official title of The Knights of St Francis. It first met at his London home in Hanover Square, switched to the George & Vulture pub and then to the dilapidated St Mary's Abbey at Medmenham, Buckinghamshire. Dashwood repaired and redesigned the building, adding a Gothic tower. Over the doorway he carved the motto 'Fais ce que tu voudras'. ('Do what thou wilt.') In the abbey's interior, several statues of Venus were placed, and underneath he built 'Hellfire caves' where the member 'monks' took their mistresses for what was known as 'private devotions.' Most of the social activity was of the type enjoyed in the original club with the addition of pagan cults, such as the Druids, and more debauchery. Members, who addressed one another as 'brother,' included John Wilkes, who became the Lord Mayor of the City of London, and among the many guests was the distinguished writer Horace Walpole, the Earl of Oxford.

Jacobite Rebellions

The Act of Union in 1707 merged the English and Scottish parliaments, ending Scotland's political independence since its representatives became members of the parliament in London that also included Wales. Many, known as Jacobites or Jacks, resisted and tried to restore the Stuart monarchy. The succession of George I and the House of Hanover seemed to end this, having been arranged by the Protestant Whigs, who opposed the Catholic Stuarts and their Tory supporters. However, an immediate Jacobite uprising happened in 1715 in Scotland. That

OPPOSITE: Londoners were shocked by the riots growing out of political tavern clubs that pitted supporters of King George against those of the Stuart pretender, James. After five executions of rioters, the mug-house violence stopped.

ABOVE: Although he created his Hellfire Club, Sir Francis Dashwood loved art and architecture, being a founding member of the Dilettante Society, and was a famous politician. Benjamin Franklin was thought to have visited his caves.

RIGHT: The Battle of Culloden ended the Jacobite rebellion and was the last ever full-scale battle in Britain. English troops then hunted and killed Scots in the Highlands, but Charles escaped to the Isle of Skye and then France.

summer, John Erskine, the Earl of Mar, raised a force of clans and marched to Perth to confront the Duke of Argyll's smaller army at the Battle of Sheriffmuir on 13 November. The battle was drawn, but Erskine's men then melted away.

Further Jacobite rebellions occurred, one in 1719 in the Scottish Highlands that was crushed, and the last in 1745 when the young pretender Charles Edward Stuart, later known as 'Bonnie Prince Charlie,' landed in northern Scotland and used his daring and charm to rally Highlanders. They marched to Derby and won the Battle of Falkirk on 17 January, but Charles Edward Stuart's troops refused to go further. They returned to be utterly defeated by the Duke of Cumberland on 16 April at the Battle of Culloden near Inverness. The English brutally killed their wounded enemy, executed 120 and transported some 1000 prisoners overseas. Charles was hunted for months and barely escaped to Europe. To all intents and purposes, the Jacobite risings were over.

The South Sea Bubble

The South Sea Company was established in 1711 to trade with South America. Its business was a public-private company intended to reduce a portion of the government's debt by providing funds for the Bank of England and the East India Company. It dealt largely by shipping slaves to Spanish America and, although only moderately successful, the company announced in 1720 it would take over the majority of the government's debt. This created a flurry of investment in its shares that were paying 100 per cent interest. Their price boomed from £128 to £1000 by June 1720, and other 'bubble' companies emerged to deal in wild investments. In September, the South Sea Bubble burst and many of the nation's prominent people, including its governor King George I, lost large amounts of money. Many were bankrupt or had their reputations ruined, including those whose shady dealings helped create the bubble in the first place. The government's

The South Sea Bubble created misery for dealers and speculators. This scene, imagining the chaos that must have been, was painted by the Victorian painter Edward Matthew Ward and hangs in London's Tate Gallery.

bailout cost it about £4 million of debt (a small part still being paid off three centuries later). An inquiry found three government ministers had taken bribes to promote the company in parliament and that company directors had fraudulently manipulated the stock for their own profit. Several were imprisoned or had their estates confiscated.

Cabinet government had begun under George I, and Sir Robert Walpole became the first Prime Minister, although the title was not used. He had opposed government involvement in the company, and when the bubble burst he was able to mitigate some of the damage in his second role of First Lord of the Treasury.

The disaster led to many restrictions on how companies could be formed. The South Sea Company sold most of its rights to the Spanish government in 1750 and continued in business for another century until 1853.

BELOW: George Cruikshank engraved these images for William Harrison Ainsworth's bestselling 1839 novel, *Jack Sheppard*. It depicts Jack being saved from the gallows by his fellow robber Joseph 'Blueskin' Blake and the mob carrying him away.

Jack Sheppard's Farewell to Mr Wood.

Blueskin cutting down Jack Sheppard.

The body of Jack Sheppard carried off by the Mob.

The Escapes of Jack Sheppard

Born in poverty in Spitalfields, young Jack Sheppard served as a carpenter's apprentice, but soon decided his true talents lay in robbery. Only 1.6m (5ft 4in) tall and slightly built, he was easy to arrest but difficult to hold, which ensured his image as a romantic hero among Londoners. Four times in one year he made amazing escapes from custody.

Arrested for theft on April 1724, he was held in St Giles Roundhouse, but broke through the roof and escaped, throwing tiles down on his guards. The next month he was arrested for pickpocketing and imprisoned along with his prostitute lover, Elizabeth Lyon, in New Bridewell Prison in Clerkenwell. There, Jack filed off his fetters, knocked a hole in the wall, removed an iron bar from the window and abseiled with Bess on rope made from his bed sheet. They then scaled a 6.7m (22ft) wall to freedom.

Captured on 23 July, he was sentenced to death for burglary and held in Newgate Prison. Bess and another prostitute visited and distracted the guard while Jack used a file Bess had smuggled in, and he escaped wearing one of her dresses. While on the lam this time, he wrote a letter to the executioner, Jack Ketch, regretting that he could not join the two other criminals scheduled to be hanged with him. Saying he was drinking to Ketch's health, Sheppard thanked him for 'the favour you intended me this day' and closed with, 'dear Jack, you find that bars and chains are but trifling obstacles in the way of your Friend and Servant.'

Caught again in September, he was taken to Newgate Prison, placed in manacles and chained to the floor of a special strongroom. No problem for Jack, who slipped out of his manacles and used a nail to pick the locks that held him to the floor, then climbed up a chimney, picked his way through several more locked doors and pushed through a grille to the roof. He then went back to his cell for a blanket, which he used to slide onto the roof of a house allowing him to walk through to exit via the front door while still wearing his leg irons, which were soon removed by a shoemaker. He then immediately went to rob a pawn shop, taking a sword, a gentleman's suit and snuff box so he could shock his friends dressed as an aristocrat.

After a fortnight of open drinking, Jack was arrested by the infamous Jonathan Wild, the 'Thief-taker General.' The public could visit him in Newgate, and hundreds arrived each day and paid four shillings for the pleasure. He even had his 'execution portrait' painted by Sir Henry Thornhill. This time, there was no escape for Jack. On 16 November 1724, a crowd of about 200,000 attended his hanging, with weeping women throwing flowers as he passed. The handsome 22-year-old nearly escaped again, but authorities discovered the penknife Jack had hidden to cut his ropes and leap to the safety of his admiring supporters. After he was hanged, the crowd surged forward to prevent the body being removed for dissection, but this action also ruined his friends' plan to see if a doctor could revive him.

Four years later, John Gay used Jack as the inspiration for his character Captain Macheath in *The Beggar's Opera*.

'A crowd of 200,000 attended his hanging, with weeping women throwing flowers.'

ABOVE: Jonathan Wild was proud of his legal position and could be seen patrolling London's streets with a silver staff of authority. Many of the thieves he caught, however, were former criminals he had been blackmailing.

The Thief-taker General

Jonathan Wild was one of London's master criminals who worked with the law to catch lawbreakers while running gangs of criminals himself. He became infamous as the 'Thief-taker General.'

Wild was born in Wolverhampton, Staffordshire, but deserted his wife and child for the illicit excitements of London. He ended up in debtors' prison where he made connections for his network of crime. His organization included thieves, pickpockets, highwaymen, extortionists and fences who disposed of stolen items. Victims also paid Wild for 'finding' goods that his thieves had stolen. Any among his group who resisted his power were betrayed to authorities, and estimates have been made that he was responsible for the executions of some 120 men. He also helped constables find and arrest petty thieves that frequented the city streets, and he gave evidence at their trials. The government paid him a fee of £40 for each conviction.

THE BOW STREET RUNNERS

London's first professional police force came about gradually in the eighteenth century. 'Rotational offices' were established in the 1730s with magistrates there, so members of the public could come for help. One was opened in 1739 in Bow Street, near Covent Garden, and the new practice of hiring 'thief-takers' was introduced in 1748: people who were paid retainers to track down and arrest criminals. Among the renowned trackers were Jonathan Wild, known as the 'Thief-taker General,' John Townsend and John Sayer. Members of the group became known as the Bow Street Runners, despite their official title of Principal Officers. This system was organized by Henry Fielding, a magistrate and novelist, and his half-brother, John Fielding. They also hired part-time constables to make foot and horse patrols through the city.

By 1792, London had six police offices with each made up of six constables and three magistrates, and by 1800 the Thames Police Office opened in Wapping with 100 constables and three magistrates to handle crime on the docks and river. Londoners who were used to self-policing their neighbourhoods now had professional forces looking after their safety.

RIGHT: The Bow Street Magistrates' Court with its runners. The building still stands adjacent to Covent Garden Opera House.

The public began to turn against Wild after his betrayal of the beloved Jack Sheppard, famed for his four escapes from prisons. After Wild's 15 years of working both sides of the law, officials had had enough of his criminal empire and arrested him on a minor felony charge and sentenced him to death. On the way to the gallows, his procession stopped at three taverns to allow him last drinks. He was hanged at Tyburn on 24 May 1725. The hangman had been a guest at his wedding and gave Wild extra time before the execution. A few days after his body was buried, physicians exhumed it and his skeleton can still be seen at the Royal College of Surgeons.

OPPOSITE: Jonathan Wild was carted to his execution at Tyburn and pelted with dirt and stones. He was nearly comatose, having swallowed poison in the morning, but surviving. His sluggish nature at the gallows irritated the crowd.

Jenny Diver

Born in Ireland as Mary Young, she was illegitimate and abandoned. She learned needlework in school and decided to move to London and become a seamstress. Once there, however, she fell in with a bunch of pickpockets and was so successful with her agile fingers that she became leader of the gang. They renamed her Jenny Diver, because a pickpocket was then known as a 'diver.'

RIGHT: Jenny Diver became celebrated for her criminal skills, with this publication calling her 'the Queen of pick-pockets'. Days before her execution, she gave her three-year-old child to her jailer, causing him to weep.

THE NEW

Newgate Calendar

CONTAINING THE

Remarkable Lives and Trials of Notorious Criminals, Past and Present.

No. 64.—Vol. I.   Splendidly Illustrated.   Price One Penny.

JENNY DIVER'S STOLEN INTERVIEW WITH HER LOVER.

JENNY DIVER, THE FEMALE MACHEATH, KNOWN AS THE QUEEN OF THE PICK-POCKETS.

———o———

A CHARACTER more celebrated for light-fingered depredations it would be impossible to find than the notorious woman whose exploits we are about to relate

Her depredations were executed with the courage of a man, aided by all the softer deceptions of an artful female.

Jenny Diver, or Mary Young, as we believe her right name to have been, was born in the north of Ireland.

Her parents seem to have been persons in indigent circumstances, and dying when she was an infant she had no recollection of them.

Some poor persons—nearly as poverty-stricken as her parents

Jenny always dressed in the best fashion and became adept at holding out her hand for gentlemen to assist her, then quickly removing their rings. A more creative trick was when she attended church wearing false arms and hands; sitting next to wealthy worshippers, she would pick their pockets while her bogus arms remained in front of her. In another ruse, she invited a wealthy gentleman to her bedroom. After he undressed, Jenny's fellow thief came to the door posing as a maid to announce her husband's return. The man was told to hide under the bed covers while they hid his clothes, and the gang stole all his valuables, including his diamond ring, a gold watch, the gold hilt of a sword and a gold-headed cane.

Jenny was finally caught with her hand in a gentleman's pocket in 1733. She was sentenced to be executed, but this was reduced to transportation to Virginia. She became bored in America and soon bribed a ship's captain for passage back to Britain, an act that automatically carried a death sentence. Back on the streets with fingers no longer so nimble, Jenny was arrested again. She used the alias of Jane Webb, and so this was recorded as a first crime and in 1738 she was again transported to America. Again she bribed her way back and resumed her trade. When she attempted to pickpocket a woman's purse on 10 January 1741, the victim noticed and held her hand tightly until others assisted and found a constable.

Jenny and her accomplice, Elizabeth Davies, 'pleaded their belly' saying they were pregnant, which doctors disproved. Elizabeth was sentenced to be transported, but the court had discovered Jenny's return from America and her previous trials under assumed names, so she was given the death sentence. On 18 March, she was taken with 19 other prisoners to Tyburn for a mass hanging, dressed in a fine black dress and a hat with a veil. It was recorded that she died quickly.

> **'They renamed her Jenny Diver, because a pickpocket was then known as a "diver".'**

Anti-Irish Riots

The Irish had long been coming to London for work, but their numbers increased rapidly in 1736. This angered locals as jobs went to the newcomers who were willing to accept lower wages. Builders of a new church in Shoreditch, for instance, let many of their local workers go and replaced them with Irishmen, paying them half the English wage.

On 26 July, riots against the Irish began in Shoreditch and Spitalfields, where Irish weavers were taking over, then quickly spread to Whitechapel, Lambert, Southwark and other areas. The mobs yelled that they were out of work and

LAVINIA FENTON

The illegitimate daughter of a naval lieutenant, Lavinia Fenton became a child prostitute at a time when a virgin's price was around £150 and brothels dealt in children as young as 10. Lavinia had better things in mind and became a street singer near her mother's coffee house in Charing Cross. Beautiful and vivacious, she became an actress in 1726 and went on to fame two years later at the age of 20, creating the role of Polly Peacham in John Gay's *The Beggar's Opera*. William Hogarth painted her in a scene from the production. That same year, Lavinia abandoned her career to run away with the married Charles Paulet, Duke of Bolton, to become his mistress for 23 years, and they had three sons. After his wife died in 1751, they wed and Lavinia became a duchess.

RIGHT: Lavinia Fenton married into a title, but was never accepted by her in-laws and other aristocrats.

starving because of the Irish. About 4000 rioters marched through the streets and attacked the obvious targets – Irish pubs – breaking windows and gutting the interiors. The militia and Tower guards were called out and the troublemakers put down. Over the following days, however, mobs would appear here and there hunting for people with Irish accents and asking others if they supported the Irish or the English. The riots died away after the middle of August, but prejudice against the Irish lingered on.

A Haven for Harlots

An estimate of prostitution in eighteenth-century London said one in five young women chose or were forced into this profession. The business was centred around Covent Garden, nicknamed 'the Square of Venus' by the magistrate Sir John Fielding. Coffee houses, taverns and gin shops were often meeting places. Most worked as streetwalkers in the East End of the city and its docks; more expensive courtesans lived in fine homes in the west, such as Marylebone and Soho. Sex in parks and other public places was not uncommon. Many prostitutes were close to poverty, but some earned as much in a month as a clerk did in a year. Such a 'lady of pleasure' could earn over £400 a year compared to a housemaid's £5 annually. *Harris's List of Covent Garden Ladies* was a small book listing and describing prostitutes, complete with their addresses. First published in 1757, it continued for more than 30 years.

Reformers and societies for 'the suppression of vice' made an effort to reduce prostitution, but Londoners were mostly tolerant of the sex trade. Magdalen

> ## 'Some prostitutes earned as much in a month as a clerk did in a year.'

CHARLOTTE HAYES

The daughter of Elizabeth Ward, who kept a brothel, Charlotte went into the same business as a teenager, managing houses in Soho and then St James's, choosing the new surname of Hayes. She spent more than she earned, however, and had several stays in debtors' prisons. In Fleet Prison in 1756, she met a professional gambler, Dennis O'Kelly, and became his mistress when they were released after George III gave amnesties to imprisoned debtors.

Charlotte now opened a luxury four-storey brothel in King's Place near to St James's Palace, where customers would pay up to £100 for a night's stay. She claimed to have the 'choicest goods,' and her most renowned acquisition was Emily Warren, who became a famous courtesan. Charlotte also provided male prostitutes for women. Visitors to London were amazed at the line of coaches in front of Charlotte's place of business, and she eventually went on to run several brothels in London.

Her lover, meanwhile, struck it lucky buying a stallion, Eclipse, that became a champion racehorse, winning 18 races and bringing £3000 in prize money. Between their two enterprises, the couple accumulated enough to buy several properties worth a total of £70,000. After O'Kelly died in 1785, Charlotte's health and finances declined, and she was again returned to debtors' prison in 1798. O'Kelly's nephew bailed her out after she signed over all her remaining assets to him. She died in 1813.

House was established by city merchants for penitent prostitutes, being a mixture of prayer, work and instruction. It claimed a two-thirds success rate reforming the 14,000 or so women residing there from 1758 to 1916.

Press Gangs

European and American wars in the eighteenth century required additional British troops, and when enlistments failed to raise the manpower, the army and navy restored to impressments that used physical force to meet their requirements. Those men hired by the Impress Service for this rough work were known as 'gangers.' Press gangs roamed the streets of London and other towns hunting for fit men aged 18 to 55, although these limits were often violated. Most victims were in the merchant fleets or had once served in the army or navy. Gangers could legally board merchant ships looking for men, so some captains had special hiding places for their best crewmen. The gangs were also not shy about abducting labourers and other strong-bodied civilians from the streets. Some victims were financially able to bribe press gangs to release them, and locals often fought with gangers who had seized someone in the neighbourhood.

Another method used was crimping houses – low-class boarding houses

ABOVE: **Prostitution was rife during the eighteenth century. The public did not always regard the profession with disgust, with stories written about poor girls forced to use sex to survive and perhaps find a good husband.**

where men were tricked by 'crimps' who plied them with liquor before pressing them into one of the forces. The houses were also used to keep those already taken before they were handed over. In 1794, one imprisoned man held in a house near Charing Cross for the East India Company tried to break free through a skylight and fell to his death, causing riots that led to the destruction of several crimping establishments.

Those who were pressed into military services had no recourse. The practice dated back centuries, and parliament gave its approval by passing acts in 1703, 1705, 1740 and 1749. Annual recruitment acts also gave magistrates the power to press the unemployed.

The War of 1812 between Britain and the United States was primarily due to the impressments of American sailors by the Royal Navy on the high seas in the late eighteenth century and early nineteenth century.

Transportation of Criminals

Transporting criminals overseas began in 1717 under 'the Bloody Code' as a cheap way of removing undesirables from society. Even those facing execution, especially for street crimes, might have their sentences reduced to transportation. Prisoners were first primarily sent to penal colonies in America, normally for seven years or life. From 1718 to 1776, some 50,000 convicts were transported to areas that are now Virginia and Maryland. This option ended when the American War of Independence began in 1775, and by 1787 British justice had chosen distant Australia, first to New South Wales. The journey could take six months, and early trips in creaky old warships sometimes led to the death of one in three convicts. From 1787 to 1857, some 162,000 lawbreakers were shipped to that nation, ranging from the ages of nine to over 80.

> **'Alcohol was one way the working classes of London could forget their troubles.'**

The system often snared dubious 'criminals,' such as political prisoners, like Irish nationalists, or those with trivial records who were needed for cheap labour, since prisoners were used for heavy work such as on roads, farms and in quarries. They mostly had to serve sentences from seven to 14 years, but good behaviour could reduce this by a 'ticket of leave.' Those given absolute pardons could return to Britain, but not those with conditional pardons.

Transportation continued until 1868, but had little effect on London's crime rate. Australians were objecting to receiving more criminals and the British public saw no need to give criminals a free trip to start a new life when others had to pay, so the policy was ended.

The Gin Act

OPPOSITE: Alexander Johnson's 1858 painting 'The Press Gang,' shows the brazen public seizure of men by sailors to man their ships. London's docks and port cities were favourite hunting grounds of the feared abductors.

Alcohol was one way the working classes of London could forget their troubles. Gin was introduced from the Netherlands in 1688 to a population used to beer and ale. The gin was cheap and unlicensed and uncontrolled, unlike beer and ale, so it became more and more popular with the poor. The city had over 1500 distillers in 1734 and six years later the drink was available in an estimated 9000 gin shops throughout London, leading to widespread drunkenness. Authorities worried that this habit led to laziness, poverty, apathy, vice and general crime, so they introduced duties and licensing for gin in 1729. These were increased in 1736 with harsh penalties added for violation, and this led to much rioting

ABOVE: **William Hogarth's 'Gin Lane' engraving was meant to show the dangers of drinking cheap gin. Its consumption was blamed for destitution and a multitude of crimes.**

in the city in 1737. This was controlled but little was done to enforce the new laws. The measures were dropped seven years later, and crime increased rapidly. Parliament's 'felony committee' said it was due to the consumption of gin and passed the Gin Act of 1751, which greatly increased controls on distilling.

That year, Henry Fielding, a London magistrate and novelist, wrote that gin was 'the principal sustenance (if it may be so called) of more than a hundred thousand people of this metropolis. Many of these wretches there are, who swallow pints of this poison within the twenty-four hours; the dreadful effects of which I have the misfortune every day to see, and to smell too.' The public fear about the effects of gin was also reflected in William Hogarth's contemporary engravings of emaciated Londoners on 'Gin Lane' contrasted with healthy ones on 'Beer Lane.'

Sales decreased after the Gin Act came into effect, and they were also affected by an increase in the brewing industry.

Raising a Stink

Eighteenth-century London still required a strong stomach to live among the stench of raw sewage running down uncovered drains on many streets. Added to this were droppings of the many horses at work, rotting rubbish left outside houses and the continuing practice of residents emptying their chamber pots from windows. The stink was increased by butchers and slaughterhouses tossing out the innards of animals, as well as the putrefying bodies of various animals that had died natural deaths. Rain made the streets worse, with passing carriages splashing pedestrians not from puddles of water but from cesspools. More rancid smells came from the polluted Thames, the black smoke of coal fires and even from communal graves for the poor that were covered with loose boards until filled with several layers of wooden coffins, sometimes six across and 12 deep. Ministers often held funeral services a distance from the grave to avoid the stench that arose from it. Smells were taken inside, as well. To mask the foul odours of accused commoners, fragrant flowers and herbs were often scattered around courtrooms.

'Ministers often held funeral services a distance from the grave to avoid the stench.'

BELOW: London's overcrowded streets were a dangerous mixture of noxious cesspools, rancid smells and other forms of pollution. Different classes of society mingled together to create a breeding ground for ill health and life-threatening diseases.

Dick Turpin

One of England's most celebrated highwaymen was Dick Turpin, who operated in and around London. Although brutal and unattractive, his face scarred by smallpox, Turpin is today lauded as a gallant and romantic robber of the open road. No police were assigned to protect highways in his time except some 50 or so who watched the roads into London.

ABOVE: Despite the romanticized idea of Dick Turpin as a daring highwayman, he was an unsavoury criminal figure on the road who robbed travellers and tortured women. His cool swaggering actions on the gallows reinforced his dashing image.

Turpin apparently first worked as an apprentice to a butcher in Whitechapel, now part of London. After some early petty crime, he and his Essex Gang robbed farmhouses, often torturing women for their valuables. By 1735, London newspapers were reporting on the crimes of Turpin and his men, and King George offered £50 for their capture. The next year they robbed a farmhouse at Mary-le-Bone (now London's Marylebone) and beat the farmer's wife and daughter until the farmer gave up his possessions.

'The butcher cut off his head and threw it in the Thames, then cut up his body.'

Turpin then teamed up with another infamous highwayman, Tom King, and they camped in Epping Forest, robbing those who passed by. In 1737, a gamekeeper tracked them to their hideout, seeking the bounty that was now raised to £100, but was shot dead by Turpin. When the two outlaws returned to Whitechapel, Tom King was captured by constables and when Turpin tried to shoot the officers, he fatally shot King instead. Knowing the danger of remaining in the London area, Turpin went to Yorkshire, taking the name of John Palmer and living like a country gentleman with occasional breaks for cattle rustling and highway robbery.

Turpin's fatal mistake was to shoot the cockerel of his landlord for fun. Arrested, he was held in York Castle while constables investigated stories of the so-called John Palmer stealing horses and sheep. Turpin wrote to his brother asking him to send character references from London that would help his case. His brother, however, refused the letter because sixpence postage was due and returned it to the post office where Turpin's former schoolmaster happened to be. He recognized the handwriting and Turpin was convicted and sentenced to be hanged. To prepare for the event he bought a new outfit and hired five mourners. Riding in a cart to the York racetrack for his execution, Turpin bowed to the crowds. On the gallows, he bowed to the ladies and chatted to the executioner and guards for 30 minutes before suddenly throwing himself off to hang. After he was buried, a labourer dug up his corpse to illegally sell to a surgeon for dissection. Hearing this, an angry mob descended on his office and recovered the body for a proper burial.

Turpin's image as a valiant and dashing highwayman is due to a Victorian novel written 50 years after his death. It wrongly claimed he made an epic ride from Westminster to York in less than 24 hours on a horse named Black Bess, but this had actually been done by a different highwayman, John (also William) Nevison. The legend was quickly repeated in other publications and told around the country, this adding credibility to the tale over time.

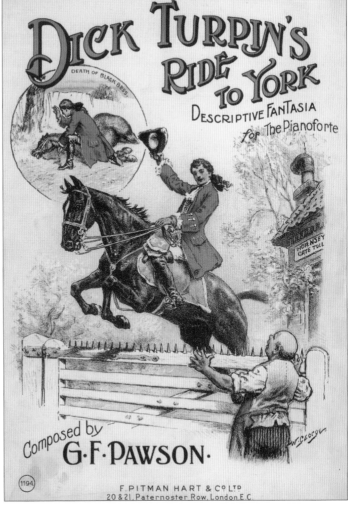

ABOVE: Turpin's heroic exploits were repeated around the country and magnified with each telling. His invented ride to York was perpetuated in the Victorian novel *Rookwood*, as well as magazines and the above music.

Wives Who Murdered

Ten women were burned at the stake at Tyburn between 1702 and 1734. Eight were found guilty of high treason for being involved with counterfeiting, and two for murdering their husbands.

Catherine Hayes worked as a prostitute and domestic servant before marrying John Hayes, the son of a Worcester farmer who employed her as a housemaid. She persuaded her husband to move to London in 1719, which gave her opportunities for affairs, including one with her illegitimate son by the farmer. Her husband was now boring her (although she claimed to have had 14 children with him), so Catherine convinced her son and another lover, a butcher, to kill him. They did so with an axe on 1 March 1726 as he lay drunk in bed. The butcher cut off his head and threw it in the Thames, then cut up the body and tossed it into a pond.

The head washed up in Westminster and authorities placed it on a spike hoping someone would recognize the victim. At least three did, and when constables went to the Hayes house they discovered Catherine in bed with her son. The remains of her husband were soon found, and all three suspects arrested.

At her trial, Catherine confessed that she only held a candle while the men did the deed, but the jury found all guilty on 30 April. The two men were sentenced to be hanged and their corpses placed in chains, but Catherine, convicted of petty treason (killing a husband), was sentenced to be burned. Awaiting her execution, she told a pastor her husband was so cruel and blasphemous 'it was no more sin to kill him than a dog or cat.'

On 9 May 1726, she was pulled on a hurdle (a panel weaved from thin branches and drawn behind a horse) to Tyburn. After praying, she was chained to the stake and a rope put round her neck through a hole in the post so she could be strangled first to avoid the pain of the fire. When the executioner lit the bundles of dry wood at her feet, however, the flame was too hot for him to strangle Catherine, and she suffered an agonizing and lengthy death, although he threw a piece of wood that broke her skull, spilling out her brains. She was reduced to ashes in an hour.

Marriage was not easy for many women in the eighteenth century. Domestic violence was viewed as a personal family affair, and self-defence was no excuse for killing an abusive husband.

Susannah Broom was an obedient wife, but suffered more than 40 years of violent abuse from her husband. Neighbours knew this was happening, seeing her bruised and bloody face and arms, but they felt helpless to intervene. The beatings usually happened when her husband returned home drunk, so Susannah began to lock him out after his drinking sessions. On one fatal night when she finally allowed him in, he began striking her. With impulsive rage, she grabbed her penknife and stabbed him in the chest, stomach and legs. Neighbours heard his cries but kept out of it, probably feeling justice was being done. The next morning, Susannah fled to her sister's home in Burford, Oxfordshire, but was quickly apprehended.

At her trial, neither she nor her neighbours were allowed to defend her actions. Susannah, 67, was found guilty and sentenced to be burned at the stake at Tyburn, which was carried out on 21 December 1739.

BELOW: Catherine Hayes died an agonizing death at the stake, giving three dreadful shrieks. During her execution, scaffolding built for 150 spectators near Tyburn collapsed twice, killing five or six people and wounding several others.

Elizabeth Brownrigg

Valued as an excellent midwife, Elizabeth Brownrigg lived a proper and admired life with her husband, a plumber. Because of this, the London Foundling Hospital allowed her to have several young girls as apprentice domestic servants. Elizabeth, however, proved to be a tyrant who meted out cruel punishments for the slightest mistakes. She would force her charges to be naked and chained by the neck to beams or pipes in order beat them with whips, canes and sticks. She also starved them and at night locked them in the coal cellar.

Two of her charges finally escaped back to the safety of the hospital, but one was returned to the Brownriggs. The governors only instructed Elizabeth's husband to restrain her punishments.

Mary Clifford, who was 14, was not so lucky. Elizabeth would tie her naked to a water pipe, hands above her heads, for beatings. The wounds Mary received from May 1766 to August 1767 became infected and she died. Elizabeth, her husband, James, and son, John, were tried for murder and Elizabeth was found guilty. Her husband and son were imprisoned for allowing the torture and for sometimes beating the girl. On 14 September 1767, Elizabeth, 47, was hanged at Tyburn before a large and hostile crowd. Her body was then dissected in public and her skeleton put on display at the Royal College of Surgeons in order that 'the heinousness of her cruelty might make the more lasting impression on the minds of the spectators.'

WHEN LONDON FOUGHT THE CITY OF LONDON

The old City of London has always protected its independence and freedoms within its Square Mile, considered separate from the rest of the capital. This rivalry came to a head in 1770 when Lord North became Prime Minister and tried to stop newspapers from publishing the proceedings in parliament. John Wilkes helped devise a plot to lure government agents into the City of London to arrest a journalist. When they did, City officials arrested the agents for assault, saying they had no jurisdiction in the Square Mile. The Westminster government responded by imprisoning Brass Crosby, the City's Lord Mayor, in the Tower of London. Soon afterwards a mob stopped the carriage of Lord North, ordered him out, grabbed his hat and chopped it into pieces that were later sold as souvenirs. While he suffered this indignity, the mob wrecked his carriage.

Resistance over the issue continued until 1774 when Wilkes became the City's mayor. That year, parliament finally decided to have its proceedings published.

LEFT: This image of Lord Mayor Crosby and Alderman Oliver imprisoned in the Tower was published in the contemporary *Oxford Magazine*.

The Massacre of St George's Fields

John Wilkes was a Member of Parliament and a journalist who criticized George III and his ministers in his newspaper, *The North Briton*. Charged with seditious libel, he was released and spent the next 15 years campaigning for the reform of parliament. 'Wilkes and liberty' became a popular cry. He was expelled from that body several times, but always re-elected. He was admittedly a radical and notorious rake who also published obscene poetry.

In 1768, Wilkes was again jailed, this time for 22 months in the King's Bench Prison in Southwark. On the way there, his supporters halted the coach and took him to a pub for a rousing bout of drinks before he sneaked away and continued on to prison. Thousands then surrounded the building in St George's Field, demanding he be released and threatening to demolish the prison, despite Wilkes calling for restraint from his window. As the crowd chanted 'No liberty, no king,' troops moved in and fired on them, killing seven (including one young man who was not involved) and injuring 15. King George feared this was a revolution and threatened to abdicate. The day was saved when Wilkes accepted his sentence.

While in prison, Wilkes corresponded with the Sons of Liberty in Boston about the 'horrid massacre,' suggesting it had been planned by the government. During his sentence he was elected Alderman for the City of London and in 1774 as its Lord Mayor, as well as a Member of Parliament again. By then, John Wilkes Clubs had been formed in Britain and America, whose revolution he supported, to commemorate his advocacy of freedom, which he declared was for everyone, including 'all the middling and inferior sort of people who stand most in need of protection.'

Lady Worsley's 27 Lovers

London's Georgian society was scandalized by the divorce proceedings of Sir Richard Worsley and his wife, Seymour. They had married in 1775. He, 24, was a baronet and Member of Parliament; she, 16, was the daughter of Sir John Fleming, a baronet. The couple became part of

BELOW: Joshua Reynolds' full-length oil painting of Lady Worsley hangs in Harewood House in Yorkshire next to Reynolds' same-size portrait of Lord Worsley. They were painted in happier days when the house was being built.

the city's hedonistic set. They had a son in 1776, but Lady Worsley, hoping to force a divorce, ran off with their friend, Captain George Bisset, after they had a daughter. The lovers spent five days in the Royal Hotel on London's Pall Mall where a maid recognized them.

Worsley refused to divorce his wife, instead suing Bisset for £20,000 on the charge of 'criminal conversation,' determined to prove that 'unlawful sexual intercourse' had damaged his possession – his wife. Worried that this would bankrupt her lover, Lady Worsley decided to prove in court that she was not worth £20,000, revealing the salacious details of her marriage and many adulteries to the eager press and public. Her defence said she had been damaged before Bisset and her husband had encouraged her actions. She brought five lovers to testify and they said Sir Richard had encouraged her affairs and even spied at their love-making through keyholes. Journalists and others added their figures up and decided she had enjoyed at least 27 lovers. The worst evidence against the husband was a maid at a public bath, who recalled Sir Richard getting Bisset to sit on his shoulders to see his wife undressing there.

> ## 'Hunger spread through the working classes, and they took to rioting.'

The judge concluded that he had prostituted her for three or four years, and the jury awarded Sir Richard one shilling in damages. Without divorcing, the Worsleys split up and she moved to France, returning in 1797. When he died in 1805, she claimed his fortune and wed a man 21 years younger and finally had a happy marriage. The couple moved to the outskirts of Paris where she died in 1818.

The Gordon Riots

Life seemed to be improving for Catholics in 1778 when parliament passed the Catholic Relief Act, which repealed harsh anti-Catholic laws on the books that excluded them from civil rights. Two years later, however, Lord George Gordon pushed to have the new relief act repealed and return to the repressive laws. On 2 June 1780, he led some 60,000 Protestant supporters to the House of Commons to hand in a petition saying the new act threatened the Church of England. This prompted riots in the city for eight days, with attacks against Catholics in the streets, their homes and chapels. About 280 people were killed and property suffered extensive damage.

The rioters' anger turned to other issues that harmed the working classes, such as high taxes and strict laws, so they attacked the Bank of England and prisons. Especially targeted was Newgate Prison, which was stormed by some thousand rioters armed with clubs and crowbars to liberate 'their honest comrades.' George III issued a proclamation to suppress the riots, and order was finally restored by army troops sent to the troubled areas.

Two of the arrested Newgate rioters, John Glover and Benjamin Bowsey, were described as 'Black' or 'Mulatto.' They were sentenced to death, but on 30 April 1781 they and the other rioters received pardons with the understanding they would serve as soldiers on the coast of Africa. Lord George Gordon was also found not guilty of high treason and acquitted. About 20 rioters, including women, were hanged. In 1786, Gordon converted to Judaism. He was imprisoned in Newgate in 1788 for libelling the French Queen and ambassador, as well as English justice. He died in the prison in 1793.

Charles Dickens' 1841 novel *Barnaby Rudge* was set during the Gordon riots.

The Burning & Plundering of NEWGATE & Setting the Felons at Liberty by the Mob.

Published 1st July 1780 by Fielding & Walker, Pater Noster Row.

Bread Riots

A bad harvest of wheat, combined with European wars that interrupted grain imports, forced the price of bread up and caused near famine in Britain in 1795. Newspapers and authorities urged poor people to eat potatoes and cook rice pudding instead, but this was resisted. Hunger spread through the working classes, and they took to rioting around the country. In London, a mob marched to 10 Downing Street to break windows of the residence of Prime Minister William Pitt the Younger, yelling 'No war, no famine, no Pitt, no King.' On 29 October, when the King was travelling to open parliament, a crowd in St James's Park yelled, 'Give us bread! Down with George!' Stones were thrown, hitting the royal coach and breaking a window. The King was unhurt and after he had left the coach, the mob attacked and almost destroyed it. Two weeks later, Pitt had two acts passed that banned assemblies of over 50 people and introduced the death penalty for anyone resisting a magistrate who attempted to break up an illegal meeting. The famine eased by the spring of 1796. More wheat had been planted, the government conducted sales of corn and imports had also increased from the Continent.

ABOVE: The Gordon rioters attacked Catholic chapels and homes, as well as diverse targets like a distillery and the Bank of England. During the riots, King George issued an order for all 'well-disposed' people to remain inside.

NINETEENTH CENTURY

The Victorian era saw immense and rapid growth in the city's population, but for many this meant overcrowding, poverty and poor health. And with the falling social standards came alcoholism and robberies, prostitution and violent crime.

Q UEEN VICTORIA'S LONG reign saw many brilliant victories. These conquests were intensely covered by the growing press, but newspapers also headlined gruesome murders in the city streets, capped by horror stories of Jack the Ripper that spread fear among ordinary Londoners.

Assassination Foiled

One of the first sensational trials in the nineteenth century involved a plot by an Irish-born British army officer and colonial administrator, Edward Marcus Despard, to assassinate King George III and overthrow the government. Found guilty, he received Britain's last ever sentence to be hanged, drawn and quartered.

Despard was a colonel who served in Jamaica and in 1781 was assigned to Central America, where he would become Governor of the British Mosquito Coast, the Gulf of Honduras and Belize. He became involved in local immigration

OPPOSITE: London streets were never safe, but the combination of a bold serial killer and growing popular press struck fear among residents who avoided leaving home at night. Police never caught up with Jack the Ripper.

Sketch'd by a Gentleman who was permitted to take a place upon the Building, the only likeness ever taken.

COL. EDWARD MARCUS DESPARD,

disputes, granting 'men of colour' the same voting and property rights as whites, and this led to local complaints and his recall in 1790. He was imprisoned from 1798 to 1800 for unknown reasons, although possibly for supporting the Irish Rebellion.

Despard next attempted to organize an army mutiny for an uprising in London that would include assassinating the King and taking over the Tower of London and the Bank of England. The plot was leaked, and he was arrested, tried and found guilty of high treason, despite Lord Horatio Nelson – who had fought with Despard – testifying for him as 'one of the brightest ornaments in the British Army.'

On 21 February 1803, Despard and six others were executed for their crime. The merciless sentence of drawing, hanging and quartering had been reduced to hanging and posthumous beheading. Instead of drawing the prisoners to a distant gallows behind a horse, the cart circled round the Surrey County Gaol grounds where the execution would take place. Despard laughed at the humour of the pompous situation, saying 'Ha! Ha! What nonsensical mummery is this?' Before dying, he addressed the crowd estimated at some 20,000, saying, 'I wish you all health, happiness and freedom, which I have endeavoured, so far as was in my power, to procure for you, and for mankind in general.'

ABOVE: Edward Despard was hanged for trying to assassinate the King and had previously fallen out of favour for supporting minorities in Central America. Londoners were shocked when he returned with Catherine, his black wife, and their son.

The Ratcliff Highway Murders

Before Jack the Ripper, the nineteenth century crimes that most terrorized Londoners happened on the Ratcliff Highway near the docks in East London. Around midnight on 7 December 1811, Timothy Marr, a linen draper, was working late with his shop boy. Marr sent his servant girl on a short errand. She returned to find that Timothy, his wife Celia, the shop boy James Gowen and the Marrs' baby Timothy Jr., had all been murdered. The infant's throat had been cut and the others bludgeoned. A murder weapon, a bloody carpenter's maul (a two-handed hammer), had been left behind and nothing was stolen. The investigation proved a shambles. The Thames River Police were joined by watchmen and magistrates, arresting dozens of innocent people. No enemies or motive could be found for killing such an ordinary, peaceful family and their employees.

Some 12 days later, the killer struck again at the King's Arms public house just a two-minute walk from the highway, bludgeoning and slashing to death the publican, John Williamson, his wife Elizabeth and their servant Anna. Their young lodger, John Turner, wearing his nightshirt, had climbed out of his window on knotted sheets yelling 'Murder! Murder!' but the killer had escaped leaving behind a crowbar. Their 14-year-old granddaughter was found alive in her bed.

Panic swept through the neighbourhoods until three days later when John Williams, a seaman, was arrested. The murder weapon had been taken from a chest in the basement of the Pear Tree Inn where Williams was a lodger. His laundress also testified she had noticed blood on his collar. Before he could be charged, however, he committed suicide in his cell, hanging himself with his scarf. This was taken as proof of guilt, and a court declared him guilty. A large crowd was given his body to parade along the Ratcliff Highway, and they pushed it into a narrow hole at a crossroads and drove a stake into his heart.

Other investigators, however, believed the evidence was thin and the real murderer had never been caught. In their 1971 book, *The Maul and the Pear Tree*, the famed mystery writer P.D. James and police historian T.A. Critchley believe Williams did not act alone and may have been murdered in prison.

ABOVE: A reward notice offered £50 for apprehending the murderer of four in the Marrs' home. Officer Charles Horton received £10 for discovering evidence, but there was never any hard evidence against John Williams.

Debtors' Prison

Some 10,000 people were imprisoned for debt each year in the nineteenth century. Debtors could be locked up for an indefinite period and not released until the debt had been paid. Victorians generally considered debt a moral failure and a crime, and judges were harsher on working class debtors, believing they had failed to repay debts on purpose. The better classes, they felt, wanted to repay, but were hindered by larger debts. Traders could avoid jail by declaring bankruptcy.

When sent to debtors' prison, such as the Fleet in the old City of London, inmates lived more like a community, having their own committee in charge of their daily lives. The better off were housed nicely on the master's side, while the poor lived in miserable conditions on the common side.

'The infant's throat had been cut and the others bludgeoned.'

THE FLEET PRISON.

In 1824, the father of Charles Dickens, John, was imprisoned with his family in Marshalsea Prison in Southwark for a debt of £40 owed to a baker. Charles, aged 12, was withdrawn from school and had to work polishing shoes in a factory to support his family, since imprisoned debtors had to pay for their meals and rooms, often increasing their debt in the process. Some spent decades in prison; others with wealthy friends could live in decent conditions and even pay to spend time outside. Charles Dickens became a strong advocate for prison reform, and his family's experience led to terrible descriptions of Marshalsea in his serialized novel *Little Dorrit* (1855–57).

Parliament passed the Debtors Act in 1869 to abolish imprisonment, but those who did not repay their debt even though they had enough money to do so could still be jailed. This and the Bankrupt Act of 1883, providing that option for those who were not traders, gave only slight relief to debtors, with 11,427 imprisoned yearly by the beginning of the twentieth century – more than in 1869.

The Cato Street Conspiracy

At the end of the Napoleonic Wars, servicemen returned seeking employment in a Britain where industrialization was putting new stresses on the working class. Urbanization also caused discontent and unrest that led to riots. In 1816, a London radical named Arthur

OPPOSITE: The Fleet Prison was named after the Fleet stream that flowed next to it. The prison burned down in the 1666 Great Fire, was rebuilt, then destroyed in the 1780 Gordon riots, again rebuilt and closed in 1844.

LEFT: Arthur Thistlewood, the son of a Lincolnshire farmer, had visited the United States and France and was impressed with their revolutions. This inspired him to try to overthrow the British government for the sake of democracy.

EXECUTING A 12-YEAR-OLD

Victorian justice often punished children as if they were adults. In November 1829, a 12-year-old boy, T. King, was tried at the Old Bailey and sentenced to death. He lived in East Smithfield with his parents who took in 'the vilest characters' and encouraged their son to lie and steal. When seven, he was an apprentice to a chimneysweeper who dismissed him for stealing in homes where they worked. He was imprisoned until the chimneysweeper brought back the stolen items, obtaining a pardon for the boy and saving him from being transported. His parents then had him join a gang of thieves who put him down the chimney of a jeweller so he could hand the expensive items out through a window. The police came and arrested him, but the others escaped. After he was sentenced to die, the boy confessed about his involvement in other robberies and even murders.

Writing about the case on 17 November 1829, one newspaper editorialized: 'We hope the dreadful example of this wretched youth may produce a lasting warning to the world at large.' No mention was made of his parents being punished.

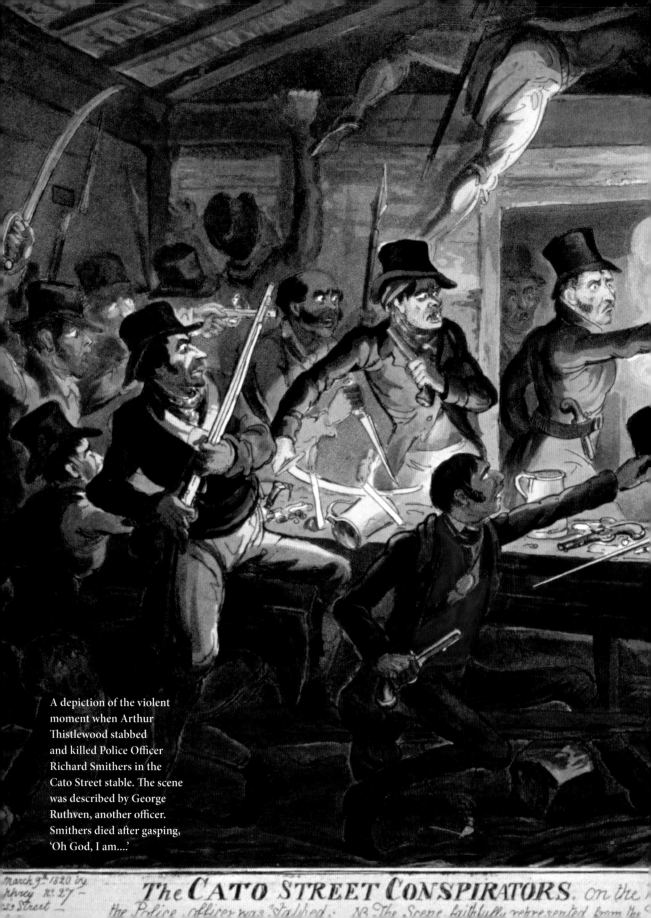

A depiction of the violent moment when Arthur Thistlewood stabbed and killed Police Officer Richard Smithers in the Cato Street stable. The scene was described by George Ruthven, another officer. Smithers died after gasping, 'Oh God, I am....'

The CATO STREET CONSPIRATORS. on the

rable night of the 23ᵈ of Febʸ 1820, at the moment when Smithers

him & Mᵗ Ruthven the View of the Interior correctl. Sketched on the Spot

Thistlewood was involved in a failed riot to seize the Bank of England and the Tower of London. He was acquitted, but in 1818 was imprisoned for his challenge of a duel to the former Prime Minister, Viscount Sidmouth, a leader who suppressed radical movements.

In 1820, Thistlewood gathered a small group together in the loft of a stable on Cato Street near Edgware Road. This time, they plotted to assassinate the entire Cabinet as they dined in the Earl of Harrowby's home in Grosvenor Square. However, the dinner was a sting devised by a police agent, George Edwards, and authorities stormed the Cato Street stable. Thistlewood killed a policeman and escaped with a sword in his hand, but was arrested the next day. One of the arrested plotters, James Ings, described how they planned to storm the dinner and murder all of the Cabinet and display the heads of Lords Castlereagh and Sidmouth on spikes at Westminster Bridge.

RIGHT: Five Cato Street conspirators became the last criminals to be beheaded by axe in England. This followed their hanging at Newgate Prison. Besides Thistlewood and Ings, the others were William Davidson, Richard Tidd and John Brunt.

THE BRIGHTON PAVILION

George IV's extravagance is most visibly seen in the opulent Brighton Pavilion. In 1815, he commissioned the architect John Nash to transform his modest villa, the Marine Pavilion, into a luxurious pleasure palace. It cost £500,000 and took seven years to create a neoclassical building that combines towers, domes and minarets into a romantic Indo-Saracenic style that has been called Brighton's Taj Mahal. The interiors were given rich decorations in the Chinoiserie style from China. The entire work, including a stable complex and flower garden, was finished in 1823. Not everyone was impressed. The contemporary writer and British politician, John Wilson Croker, opined, 'It is, I think, an absurd waste of money, and will be a ruin in half a century or more.' Today, the Royal Pavilion has retained its grandeur and welcomes 200,000 visitors a year.

LEFT: The building, officially the Royal Pavilion, is located in the centre of the popular holiday town on the English Channel.

At their trials, five conspirators were sentenced to be transported, while Thistlewood and four others were convicted of high treason (Thistlewood was also charged with murder) and condemned to be hanged and then beheaded. On the gallows on 1 May outside Newgate Prison, Ings began to sing 'Death or Liberty,' prompting Thistlewood to complain, 'Be quiet, Ings. We can die without all this noise.'

'It is, I think, an absurd waste of money, and will be a ruin in half a century.'

The King of Excess

When he became King in 1820, George IV had already ruled the country since 1811 as Prince Regent, assuming the duties of his insane father, George III. His free and extravagant ways had quickly landed him in trouble. This included a secret marriage in 1785 to the twice-married Catholic widow Maria Fitzherbert, which was an illegal union without his father's permission. In 1795, he made a deal with parliament in which he agreed to wed his cousin, Princess Caroline of Brunswick, if the government paid off his debts. He disliked his wife, keeping her away from his coronation so she could not become Queen and then attempting without success to divorce her.

George's extravagant lifestyle and immorality, including a ready supply of mistresses, embarrassed the government when wartime costs had inflicted poverty on his subjects. He especially enjoyed spectacles and expensive celebrations, which he indulged in as regent after the Duke of Wellington

RIGHT: The artist J.M.W. Turner's famous paintings of the fire that engulfed the Houses of Parliament were done from the South Bank and a rented boat on the Thames. He worked through the night to produce two oil paintings and nine watercolours.

defeated Napoleon in 1815 at Waterloo. He also created the Regency style of architecture and delighted in whimsical projects, such as the flamboyant Brighton Pavilion in that seaside resort.

Despite all this, George was intelligent, charismatic, a keen supporter of the arts and a great wit. The Duke of Wellington called him 'the most extraordinary compound of talent, wit, buffoonery, obstinacy and good feelings, in short, a medley of the most opposite qualities, with a great preponderance of good – that I ever saw in any character in my life.'

George spent his last years in the privacy of Windsor Castle. When he died in 1830, his brother succeeded him as William IV since George's daughter, Princess Charlotte, born in 1796, had died in childbirth in 1817.

The Burning of Parliament

On the evening of 16 October 1834, both Houses of Parliament were destroyed when Westminster Palace went up in flames. The only major section remaining was Westminster Hall because of valiant efforts by firemen and volunteers and a lucky change in wind direction at midnight. During the conflagration, soldiers held back hundreds of thousands of onlookers. The artist J.M.W. Turner was on the scene and did two oil paintings of the fire.

The tragedy began after workmen burned two cartloads of used wooden tally sticks (used for accounting) in two stoves in the basement. This was done in the

'During the conflagration, soldiers held back hundreds of thousands of onlookers.'

morning and by the afternoon a housekeeper noticed heat and smoke from the floor that, turned out to be a smouldering chimney. The stoves were put out at 5 p.m., but an hour later the fire erupted, soon exploding over the building in a great fireball that lit up the London sky. Prime Minister William Lamb would call this 'one of the greatest instances of stupidity on record.' Damage was estimated at £2 million. No one died and no one was prosecuted, but an inquiry found a few guilty of negligence.

The government found temporary quarters until parliament's New Palace of Westminster, begun in 1840, was opened in 1860. It was created by the architect Charles Barry and the designer A.W.N. Pugin, who devised the Clock Tower to hold the giant bell, Big Ben.

The Legend of Sweeney Todd

Sweeney Todd, whose real name was Benjamin Barker, was first introduced to readers in 1846 in *The String of Pearls: A Romance*, one of the popular 'penny dreadfuls' – sensational fiction sold in episodes each week for one penny. Many Londoners believed there was a factual basis for the story of a barber who murdered his clients and gave their meat for use in his neighbour's pie shop. No criminal records have ever been found, but the legend has endured.

ABOVE: The original 18-part series of Sweeney Todd stories was primarily written by James Rymer and Thomas Preckett, prolific writers of 'penny dreadfuls,' but others later contributed. An instant hit, it was quickly expanded into a book.

In this 18-part story, Todd's barbershop was supposedly at 186 Fleet Street. When his customers were seated, he would pull a lever causing them to flip backwards and down a trap door into the basement. If the fall did not kill them, Todd would hurry down with his straight razor and slit their throats. He then carried their bodies via a tunnel to Mrs Lovett's pie shop where the flesh was baked in a pie for her customers.

Todd's story has often been retold, including a play in 1973, a musical in 1979 and a movie in 2007.

Mrs Robinson's Diary

One would think a wife's detailed diary account of her extramarital affair was enough evidence for a divorce, but Isabella Hamilton Robinson outwitted her husband and a jury to stay married.

The couple had wed in 1844, she being a wealthy widow with a child. Henry Robinson, a civil engineer, discovered the incriminating diary in 1858 when they were living in France and his wife was bedridden with diphtheria. Her journal described her torrid affair with a doctor, Edward Lane. Even though Henry had produced two children with a mistress, he was infuriated at reading the revelations, such as Isabella's evening 'full of passionate excitement, long and clinging kisses, and nervous sensations.' He took custody of their two children and threw her out, intending to end their 14-year marriage.

Their case in 1858 in the new Court of Divorce and Matrimonial Causes in Westminster Hall was the 11th petition filed under a new law that granted divorce

'He carried their bodies to Mrs Lovett's pie shop where the flesh was baked in a pie.'

DEATH TAKES A RIDE

London's population doubled in the first half of the nineteenth century, and the city was running out of burial sites. The London railway that opened on 13 November 1854 offered trips that nobody wanted to take. The London Necropolis Company (LNC) began the railway to carry cadavers and mourners from Waterloo to its newly opened Brookwood Cemetery 40km (25 miles) southwest of the city at Brookwood in Surrey. When it opened that year, the cemetery's 2000 acres comprised the largest ground for burials in the world. Up to 60 coffins were carried on the one train that ran each day, with three classes of funerals offered.

The last Necropolis train ran in 1941, when its London terminus was bombed that April by German warplanes, but special trains continued to make the trip until after 1945. The cemetery today, still the largest in the UK, has had nearly 235,000 burials.

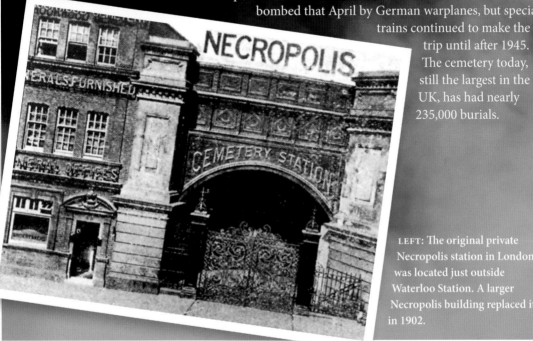

LEFT: The original private Necropolis station in London was located just outside Waterloo Station. A larger Necropolis building replaced it in 1902.

FAKE ADULTERY

Victorian couples who both wished to end their marriage had a problem: the law did not allow them to divorce just because they had grown apart or had irreconcilable differences. The one sure road to divorce was adultery, or in some cases the pretence of adultery. Judges had difficulty stopping a sham affair from wrecking a marriage. When one of the spouses was willing to risk public disgrace, a staged adultery scene was photographed as evidence. This normally involved the husband hiring a woman to be his 'mistress' and the two being in a bed when his wife burst in with a photographer. In some cases, the man was fully dressed and wore a top hat.

for adultery. Before that, divorce was expensive, requiring an act by parliament. The Robinsons' case became a lurid scandal that delighted London newspapers. Isabella's defence was insanity that caused her to write the fictional diary that she had begun in 1849. Her lawyer said she suffered from nymphomania, erotomania and a 'uterine disease' that created lustful feelings and 'sexual delusions of the most extravagant nature.' For his part, the doctor claimed he never 'put arm round her waist, or embraced her, or tempted or caressed her.'

Her testimony saved the marriage and reputation of her fictionalized (or real) lover, Doctor Lane. The two had spent time together at his spa estate with his family and patients. Her husband's decision to drag their sordid lives through the press resulted in the divorce not being granted. However, they were divorced in 1864 when Isabella was caught having an affair with a young Frenchman who had been her children's tutor.

ABOVE: London's new sewer system opened in 1865 was designed by Joseph Bazalgette, the chief engineer of the city's Metropolitan Board of Works. His river embankments opened in 1870 reclaimed ground for gardens and roads.

The Great Stink

London was the world's largest city in 1858 with a population of some 2.3 million, and its old problem of nauseating smells became unbearable that scorching July and August. The main cause of the 'Great Stink' was the introduction of water closets in better homes, so that sewers intended for rainwater now took raw sewage into the Thames where it mixed with industrial runoff. Water companies then recycled the polluted water for their customers, increasing the smell and a danger of cholera. In the oppressive summer of 1858, the hottest on record, the sun began to ferment and cook the toxic waste along the riverbanks. The stench became so bad, authorities had the curtains of the newly built House of Commons soaked with chloride and lime to mask the foul odours. The desperate members, often holding handkerchiefs over their noses, rushed through a bill in 18 days to fund one of the century's greatest engineering projects. A massive new sewer system of 133km (83 miles) was built on both sides of the river to trap the sewage and direct it east of London to pumping stations that then sent it on the ebb tides into the sea. The first sewer section was opened in 1865. Embankments were also placed along the river to ease the flow of water. The city's death toll dropped dramatically as a result, and epidemics of cholera (1832, 1848–49, 1854 and 1866) and other diseases were eventually curtailed.

'She suffered from nymphomania, erotomania and a "uterine disease".'

The Great Fraud of 1873

In the most costly and audacious robbery in nineteenth-century Britain, The Bank of England was defrauded of £100,000 (worth £10 million today) in March 1873 by an American gang led by two brothers, Austin and George Bidwell. This feat and their subsequent trial caused a sensation around the world.

After a series of frauds in America, the brothers moved their criminal operations to London in 1872. Austin posed as a wealthy US railwayman, Frederick Warren, backed up by forged letters of reference and of credit. He opened a large account in the bank's branch in Burlington Gardens, Mayfair. They were joined by two other American forgers, Edwin Noyes and the Harvard-educated George McDonnell, who produced perfect bogus promissory notes. They were cashed and the money laundered through another London

BELOW: The trial of the four American forgers -- Austin and George Bidwell, George McDonnell and Edwin Noyes – took place at the Old Bailey. During it, another Bidwell brother, John, tried to bribe warders to help them escape.

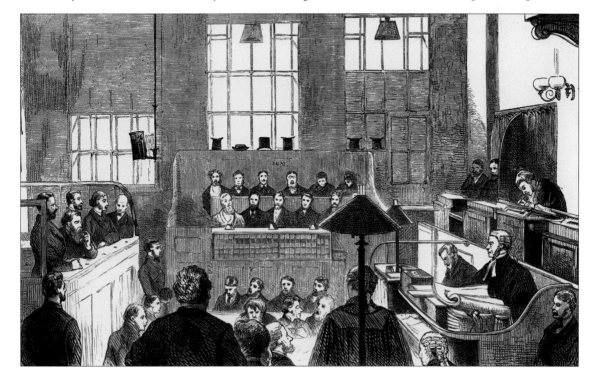

bank. When their withdrawals totalled £100,000, the money was converted to US Bonds. It would take two months for the fake promissory notes to be processed. On 28 February, Noyes made a crucial mistake when he went to a bank to turn in several notes. The clerk noted that two had no date. He contacted the person they were drawn on, and the man said they were forgeries. Noyes was arrested when he returned to the bank, and the gang fled around the world pursued by Chicago's famous Pinkerton Detective Agency. McDonnell was arrested in New York, George Bidwell in Edinburgh and Austin Bidwell in Havana, where he was run down by William Pinkerton himself.

'Forgery is a very wretched, unhappy, miserable and contemptible art, [but] an art nevertheless.'

In August 1873, their London trial, which the Lord Chief Justice called 'the most remarkable trial that ever occurred in the annals of England,' lasted eight days and heard 90 witnesses. McDonnell, for his part, remained proud of his skills, saying, 'Forgery is a very wretched, unhappy, miserable and contemptible art, [but] an art nevertheless.' The jury took 15 minutes to find them guilty, and the judge sentenced each to life. George Bidwell was released due to ill health after nearly 15 years and the others after 20 years.

Prison Hulks

The overcrowding of Victorian prisons led to the innovation of prison ships popularly known as hulks. These old, rusty vessels could be seen on the East India Docks in sharp contrast to its smart clippers. Some prisoners would serve up to 20 years on such a prison with long days of hard labour on the ship and in the

C.S. Drawn May the 8th 1777 from the BUTT at WOOLWICH

LEFT: Prison hulks had been a feature of the Thames for years. Prisoners enjoyed supervised release for outside work, and those from the countryside stayed more depressed than those in London who could see family and friends.

docks. Others were sent there to await prison ships transporting them to Australia. The unhealthy conditions spread diseases like typhoid and cholera, and many deaths occurred.

One of the hulks, the *Success*, contained 68 cells and included the 'tigers den', a loose box with bars where the most dangerous prisoners were confined together. Others were chained in their cells so they could only reach the door to receive food, which would usually be bread and water. The worst had to drag 36kg (80 lb) of chains with them when walking. This was too much weight to ascend stairs, so they had to be hauled up in a cage for fresh air.

The 'Angel Maker'

When Amelia Dyer was hanged in 1896 at Newgate Prison near the Old Bailey in London, she had become Britain's most prolific serial killer, being responsible for the deaths of some 400 babies.

She began her horrific crimes in the late 1860s in Bristol, taking in unwed mothers and keeping their babies. She would smother an infant at the mother's request or keep some and starve them to death. This developed into a fostering service in which she drugged the babies before starving them. In 1879, Amelia served a six-month prison sentence for infant neglect. When released, she devised a more profitable scheme, moving to Reading where she offered an adoption service. After receiving the parents' fee, she would kill their child.

Amelia was arrested in 1896 after an infant's body was discovered in the Thames. It was wrapped in parcel paper with Amelia's address on it. At her house, police were repelled by the stench of rotting flesh, and they found documents relating to her 'adoption' business. A further search of the river discovered about 50 more infant bodies. She told the police they would know the babies were hers, 'by the tape around their necks.'

Amelia's trial determined she had probably murdered 400 or so infants. She unsuccessfully pleaded insanity, having been twice in mental asylums in Bristol. The press dubbed her 'the Angel Maker' and songs were written about her evil deeds. The public outrage brought about stricter supervision of adoption and child-protection laws. When she was hanged on 10 June 1896 at the age of 58, authorities recorded, 'On account of her weight and the softness of the textures, rather a soft drop was given. It proved to be quite sufficient.'

The Garrotting Panic

Londoners were well aware of crimes on their streets, but this reached a panic in 1862 when more robbers were thought to assault victims by garrotting them – strangling people nearly to death. The term was quickly applied to any street mugging. The population was already worried about convicts being released early because of an overflow caused by the end of transportation overseas. The licensed prisoners were called 'ticket-of-leave men.' A few victims died, and the

ABOVE: Details of Amelia Dyer's crimes during her trial shocked the nation and boosted the importance of the National Society for the Prevention of Cruelty to Children (NSPCC) chartered in 1895, a year before her execution.

'Amelia's trial determined she had probably murdered 400 or so infants.'

OPPOSITE: *Punch* found humour in Londoners' fear of garrotting by advertising an iron collar. Another picture showed it could be worn with a suit that had protective spikes attached to the knees, heels and elbows.

fears grew after people were attacked in the supposedly secure West End. A well-publicized account in July told how Hugh Pilkinton, a Member of Parliament, was robbed on a well-lit pavement as he walked from parliament to his club in Pall Mall. That same evening, an employee of the British Museum was garotted walking between St James's and Bond Street. The panic peaked in the winter, and 23 men were convicted in November at the Old Bailey of garotting, receiving sentences from four years to life. In July 1863, parliament passed the Garotting Act that enacted the punishment of flogging for the crime

The satirical magazine *Punch* even ran advertisements for a 'patent anti-garotte collar' with the question, 'Do you wish to avoid being strangled?' It assured that the device 'enables gentlemen to walk the streets of London in perfect safety in all hours of the day or night.'

The Mordaunt Scandal

Sir Charles Mordaunt, a baronet and Member of Parliament, was happily married to the younger Harriet, a society beauty. She, on the other hand, was bored of living in Walton Hall that her husband built in 1860 for £30,000 on 4000 acres in Warwickshire.

During the summer of 1868, Charles came home unexpectedly and discovered his wife demonstrating her skills of driving a carriage with two white ponies. The problem was that her performance was for Edward, the Prince of Wales (later Edward VII), who had a reputation throughout London and elsewhere as a womanizer. Charles told the prince to leave and when he did he had his groom bring the two ponies onto the lawn below the conservatory, summoned his wife from the house and made her watch as he shot them dead.

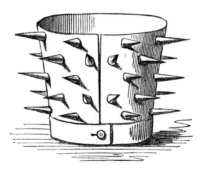

EFFECT OF THE ANTIGAROTTE COLLAR ON A GARROTTEER.

In 1870, Harriet gave birth to Violet, a blind baby. She told her husband this was due to a venereal disease and confessed that the child was not his because she had conducted many affairs – including one with the Prince of Wales. Her husband threatened to divorce her and name the prince as a co-respondent, while Harriet's parents disowned her, saying she was insane. She was taken and hidden in several houses while doctors examined her mental state. Harriet apparently faked madness, but then seemed to fall into it, chewing the carpet, eating coal and smashing china. Doctors declared her insane, and Charles sued for divorce. The Prince of Wales gave evidence, denying any sexual relationship with Harriet, but another lover admitted one (perhaps at the prince's request or payment). Harriet, 26, was placed in an asylum for the remainder of her life, dying in 1906 at the age of 58.

Charles remarried, and the blind daughter gained sight and became the 5th Marchioness of Bath.

The Dilke Scandal

Sir Charles Wentworth Dilke was a respected politician who was expected to soon lead the Liberal Party and succeed Prime Minister Gladstone. His problem was a reputation as a sexual predator, and in 1885 Donald Crawford, another Member of Parliament, named Dilke as the co-respondent in his divorce proceedings against his wife, Virginia. She was 22 and had been forced by arrangement to marry Crawford, 47. She admitted adultery without the case going to court, meaning Virginia was accused of adultery with Dilke, but he was not guilty of adultery with her. The divorce was granted. Crawford's counsel called him 'a coarse brutal adulterer more benefitting a beast than a man,' and the public still thought him guilty, jeopardizing his career.

Some 11 days before he decided to reopen the case in July 1886, Dilke lost his re-election. He was still convinced his could talk his way to

innocence at the trial. Instead, his testimony rambled and evaded, while Virginia gave specific dates, locations and even floor plans. She claimed Dilke had had many more affairs, including one with his maid. Virginia said she joined both of them in bed, and Dilke 'taught me every French vice' and that 'he used to say that I knew more than most women of 30.' She also noted that Dilke had admitted an affair with her mother and said that Virginia 'was very much like my mother' and that was why he had taken a fancy to her. Although Virginia admitted adultery, along with her sister, with medical students at a hospital and with Captain Henry Forester in a brothel, she said Dilke was her main lover.

The divorce was granted, and Dilke's rise to the top of the political world was finished. Historians in general feel he may have had some close relationship to Virginia without adultery. She may have chosen Dilke for her accusations to achieve the divorce, because he was already known as a ladies' man and she

No. 1,284.   SATURDAY, SEPTEMBER 22, 1888.   Price One Penny.

resented his affair with her mother. Dilke recovered enough to be married and once more elected to parliament, where he served until his death in 1911.

Society turned its back on Virginia, but she became a newspaper writer and a very religious Catholic. She spent many years in public service, such as nursing London's poor, and died in 1948 at the age of 85.

'The murderer cut their throats and horribly mutilated their bodies.'

Jack the Ripper

The poor Whitechapel area of East London was the scene of five murders in 1888 that were attributed to a serial killer dubbed 'Jack the Ripper' in sensational stories on the front pages of London newspapers. All the slain were prostitutes, and all but one were killed while soliciting on the streets. The murderer cut their throats and horribly mutilated their bodies with the skill of a surgeon, or a butcher with a good knowledge of anatomy.

The number of victims was uncertain. The press and some junior policemen believed the total was seven or nine. Martha Tabram, stabbed to death on 7 August, was considered by several investigators to have been the first. The five normally attributed to the Ripper were: Mary Ann Nicholls on 31 August; Annie Chapman on 8 September; Elizabeth Stride and Catherine Eddowes on 30 September; and Mary Jane Kelly on 9 November. All but Stride suffered abdominal mutilations, with Kelly's heart taken away and her injuries so brutal the press had difficulty describing them. The murderer also took away Chapman's uterus and Eddowes' uterus and left kidney.

Extra constables were put on the streets with bloodhounds, and hundreds of suspects were brought in for questioning, all to no avail. Police even used a current idea that a victim's eyes could reveal the image of the last person viewed – the murderer – but photographs of the retinas of one slain prostitute found nothing. The four main suspects named by Scotland Yard in 1889 were Aaron Kosminsky, 23, a Polish Jew living in Whitechapel who died in an insane asylum; Montague John Druitt, 31, a barrister and teacher who committed suicide in December 1888; Michael Ostrog, 55, a Russian-born thief who had been in asylums; and Dr Francis J. Tumblety, 56, an American 'quack' doctor arrested for indecency who fled the country.

During the investigations, someone claiming to be the killer sent letters to the police taunting them for failing to solve the crimes. Also, on 16 October, George Lusk, the chairman of the Whitechapel Vigilance Committee, received a cardboard box that contained half a kidney supposedly from a victim. Addressed *From Hell*, the writer claimed to have fried and eaten the other half, saying it was 'very nise.' It ended with, 'signed Catch me when you can Mishter Lusk.'

Accounts of Jack the Ripper's murders riveted readers throughout Britain, Europe and America. More than 100 books have been written about him, as well as movies and television dramas. The killer's identity remains one of the great unsolved mysteries in criminal history.

A Royal Ripper Suspect

Throughout the years, professional and amateur sleuths have suggested many names as the possible murderer. The painter Walter Sickert, who was fascinated with the killings, has long been on the list, and his guilt is believed by the American crime novelist, Patricia Cornwell. One unusual suspect often suggested has been Prince Albert Victor, the son of King Edward VII and grandson of Queen Victoria. Two of his letters held privately were auctioned in 2016. They reveal that probable contact with a prostitute had given him gonorrhoea. In 1970, a British physician, Thomas Stowell, said the prince's sexual disease had caused insanity and driven him to commit the murders. He added that the Royal family knew that Albert, known as Eddie, had killed at least two of the prostitutes. Other investigators, however, believe the evidence does not hold up.

In the 2001 movie *From Hell,* Johnny Depp plays Frederick Abberline, the real police inspector on the Ripper case, and the film suggests Prince Albert's involvement.

Oscar Wilde's Conviction

Homosexuality was a crime under British law, and its most famous 'criminal' was the brilliant writer Oscar Wilde, who had his career and liberty ended by one mistake.

Born in Dublin, Wilde was educated at Trinity College there and at Magdalene College, Oxford. He became known for his long hair and eccentric clothes, but most of all for his wit, which he displayed in 1882 lecturing in Canada and the United States. In 1884 he married Constance Lloyd, and they had two sons.

Wilde, always a great wit, became a brilliant writer, highlighted by his plays and in 1890 by his one novel, *The Picture of Dorian Gray*. In 1895, he was at the height of his fame, with his comedy, *The Importance of Being Earnest*, an enormous stage success in London. But that year he was angered by a note written by the Marquis of Queensberry, the father of Wilde's lover, Lord Alfred Douglas, a relationship he flouted openly. It accused the playwright of being a 'somdomite.' Instead of brushing off the insult, Wilde sued the man for libel, but dropped the suit when the evidence went against him. He was then arrested for gross indecency with men and became the first person prosecuted under the new homosexual law of 1885. The first jury was undecided, but a second one found him guilty. On 25 May 1895, Wilde was sentenced to two years in prison with hard labour. During his time in Reading Gaol, he became bankrupt and suffered mentally and physically.

When released in 1897, Wilde was a broken man who retreated to France and Italy, writing *The Ballad of Reading Gaol* in 1898. He ended his days in a small flat in Paris where he entertained a few friends and died in 1900.

BELOW: Oscar Wilde's relationship with Lord Alfred Douglas may have continued undisturbed if the playwright had not sued the man's father. After Wilde's release from jail, the two met again and briefly lived together in Naples.

The Cleveland Street Scandal

Charles Hammond's male brothel for aristocrats at 19 Cleveland Street off Oxford Street was a secret establishment for years before several young telegraph boys were discovered renting their services there. Homosexuality was illegal and an unspoken subject at fine London homes, so the news of eminent men engaged in sexual activities with young boys was a shocking scandal.

SLANG TERMS FOR CRIMINALS

A special language for crime existed in Victorian London's East End, where cockneys made up a good portion of the offenders. Some terms then in popular use included:

Burglar = cracksman, buster, snoozer (stealing as people slept), parlour-jumper
Cardsharp = broadsman
Confidence man = magsman
Counterfeiter = smasher
Enforcer = punisher, nobbler
Fence = duffer
Informer = blower
Mugger = rampsman
Policeman = reeler, mutton shunter
Pickpocket = dipper, mobsman, mutcher, tooler, drunken-roller
Prostitute = skittle, adventuress, toffer (attracting posh clients), dollymop (amateur or part-time), abbess (brothel madam)
Robber = huntsman
Safe-cracker = screwman
Seducer = gal-sneaker
Shoplifter = palmer
Lookout = crow, canary (if a female)

Even more specialist terms were used, such as a toy-getter for one who stole watches, a peter-claimer who stole boxes, a bludger who used bludgeons and a skinner for a woman who stripped children to rob them of their clothes.

RIGHT: Young offenders quickly picked up street cant, or slang, which they used almost as a foreign language around their victims.

The truth came out on 4 July 1889 when Charles Thomas Swinscow, 15, who delivered telegrams around the city, was stopped and questioned about a recent robbery at the General Post Office, his employer. Found to be carrying the considerable sum of 18 shillings, he was taken in for questioning. Charles quickly confessed that Hammond had recruited him for his clientele, paying him four shillings for each act. He also identified three other telegraph boys who were involved.

Officers went to the establishment to arrest Hammond for conspiracy to 'commit the abominable crime of beggary,' but he had fled and eventually emigrated to the United States and was not pursued. In September, the rent boys were found guilty of gross indecency at the Old Bailey and given sentences of four to nine months with hard labour.

Prince Albert Victor, second in line to the throne, was among those rumoured to be a client. Those accused included: Lord Arthur Somerset, who went abroad during the scandal; Henry James Fitzroy, the Earl of Euston, who successfully sued a newspaper who named him; and Colonel Jervois of the Second Life Guards. By 1890, some 60 men had been identified and 22 of them had fled abroad.

'Homosexuality was illegal and an unspoken subject at fine London homes.'

Because the leading press did not name those involved, the public soon lost interest in the scandal. Many politicians and members of society believed the government had conspired to hush up the story and protect the reputations of important people. A motion in parliament on 28 February 1890 to have a committee investigate the affair was defeated by a vote of 204 to 66.

A Transatlantic Serial Killer

Thomas Neill Cream was born in Glasgow and moved as a young boy with his family to Canada to study medicine at McGill University. He was married, but his wife died within a year of a mysterious illness. He next studied medicine in London in 1876. He opened his practice in Edinburgh and in 1879 his pregnant mistress was found dead, poisoned with chloroform. Cream was accused and fled to Chicago, where he offered cheap abortions to prostitutes. Two died, as well as the husband of his new mistress. The man was buried, but Cream wrote telegrams to the coroner saying it was foul play and the murderer was a druggist. Police soon figured out who it was. Cream was convicted of murder in 1881 and sentenced to life. Ten years later, he was released after his father died and left him enough money to bribe a prison official to agree that he was no longer dangerous.

That year, 1891, Cream moved to Lambeth in London and is known to have killed at least four prostitutes. He visited the last two, Alice Marsh, 21, and Emma Schrivell, 18, in their flat, and offered them bottles of Guinness laced with strychnine. Newspapers frightened the locals even more by headlining 'The Lambeth Poisoner.' Cream next tried to blackmail doctors and wealthy people, saying he knew of their involvement in the murders and for a price would send them the evidence to suppress. His big mistake was talking to a policeman at a party and revealing too many details about the cases. The authorities looked into his association with prostitutes and soon were in contact with the Chicago police who revealed his murder conviction.

He was arrested on 13 July 1892 for killing four prostitutes. He claimed he was Thomas Cream, not the Neill Cream jailed for murder. Officers, however,

found seven bottles of strychnine in his home. He was tried in October for the murder of one, Matilda Clover, and the jury took only 12 minutes to declare him guilty. On 15 November, he was hanged privately at Newgate Prison. Just as the trap door opened, he supposedly yelled, 'I am Jack,' taking credit for the Ripper murders. When they had happened, however, Cream was imprisoned in Chicago.

LEFT: The noose cut off the end of Thomas Cream's sentence at 'I am Jack....' The rumour persisted that he was the Ripper, with some believing he was in London because he had paid a double to serve his jail time in Chicago.

The Plaistow Horror

In the very hot July of 1895, Robert Coombes, who was 13, murdered his 37-year-old mother in their small terraced house in Plaistow (now in London's East End), while their father was off working on a ship in the Atlantic. Robert and his brother, Nathaniel, 12, remained with the body for nine days, going to Lords to watch a cricket match, fishing at Southend-on-Sea and enjoying a play at a theatre, all the while telling neighbours their mother was visiting relatives in Liverpool.

The stench of death finally became noticeable outside their house, and police found the brothers inside playing cards with a friend and Mrs Coombes' body in her bedroom crawling with maggots. Robert confessed, saying, 'My brother Nattie got a hiding for stealing some food, and Ma was going to give me one.' He added that his brother wanted to stab her but was unable, asking Robert to do the deed. Stabbing had failed, so he suffocated her with a pillow.

> ## 'The stench of death finally became noticeable outside their house.'

Newspapers dubbed the murder the 'Plaistow Horror,' with one calling it 'the most horrible, the most awful and revolting crime that we have ever been called upon to record.' Learning that Robert played the mandolin, another paper noted that 'This love of music is not infrequent among the bad folk of criminal history.'

At his trial, Robert seemed unworried about his guilt and even grinned at the proceedings, while his younger brother shook and cried. The defence blamed the murder on Robert's terrible headaches and his love for the sensation fiction of penny dreadfuls. The boy was found guilty by reason of insanity and sent for an indefinite period to Broadmoor lunatic asylum, which offered relatively humane confinement. Robert, the youngest inmate, could play cricket and join the brass band. He was released in 1912 at the age of 30 and moved to Australia, joining his brother who had lived there for years after the court decided he had not participated in the murder. During World War I, Nathaniel served in Australia's navy and Robert in its army as a stretcher-bearer who won the Military Medal.

OPPOSITE: London's sensational *Police News* gathered a large readership by displaying violent sketches of crimes. This entire front page covered the Plaistow Horror as a simplified illustrated story to reach all types of readers.

MODERN LONDON

The last two centuries have ushered in advances in technology that the Metropolitan Police have used to identify and capture lawbreakers, but science has also been employed for criminal activities, including murder.

T HE TWENTIETH CENTURY saw the fastest advances in forensic science, with databases established for fingerprints, DNA, photographs and other evidence to solve decades-old cold cases. Today, criminals try to stay one step ahead of the law using new methods, such as the internet and mobile phones.

Doctor Crippen

Hawley Harvey Crippen was an American physician who murdered his wife and fled for days before becoming the first criminal to be arrested by the use of a telegram.

Crippen had married his wife, Cora, in 1892 in New York City. In 1897, they moved to London, where he sold patent medicines and she became a music hall singer under the name of Belle Elmore. The two were contrasts in personalities, with the doctor having a meek manner and his wife being boisterous and outgoing, having several affairs. Crippen also had an affair with a young secretary,

OPPOSITE: Protests against the government's new poll tax in 1990 led to some of the largest riots in the history of London and the nation. Prime Minister Margaret Thatcher's refusal to back down resulted in her resignation.

Ethel Le Neve, whom he worked with at an institution for the deaf. In December 1909, Crippen's wife informed him that she intended to leave him and withdraw the money from their savings account. A month later she disappeared. He explained this by saying she had gone back to the United States on a visit. Later he announced she had died there. Soon after, Ethel moved into his home and was seen in public wearing Cora's furs and jewellery. Their indiscreet actions raised suspicions, and Inspector Walter Dew visited Crippen at his home in Holloway, north London. The doctor now claimed his wife had run off with another man. When Dew made a return visit, the couple had fled.

A search uncovered parts of human remains buried in a hole under the brick floor of the basement. A post mortem identified them as Cora and found that she had been poisoned before the dismemberment. While newspapers spread stories about the sensational murder, Crippen was in Brussels unaware of this turn of events as he escaped with Ethel (disguised as a boy) on a ship sailing from Antwerp to Canada. They were recognized by the captain, who telegraphed Scotland Yard. Inspector Dew took a faster ship and arrested the doctor at the

CRIPPEN'S ARREST

Having fled London, Crippen and Ethel were crossing the Atlanta on the *Montrose*, with Ethel disguised as a boy. Captain Henry George Kendall recognized the fugitives, and just before steaming beyond the range of his shipboard transmitter, he had telegraphist Lawrence Ernest Hughes send a wireless telegram to the British authorities: It read: 'Have strong suspicions that Crippen London cellar murderer and accomplice are among saloon passengers. Mustache taken off growing beard. Accomplice dressed as a boy. Manner and build undoubtedly a girl.'

ARRESTATION DU DOCTEUR CRIPPEN ET DE MISS LE NEVE SUR LE PONT DU «MONTROSE»

Had Crippen travelled third class, he probably would have escaped Kendall's notice. Walter Dew boarded a faster White Star liner, arrived in Quebec ahead of Crippen and contacted the Canadian authorities. As the *Montrose* entered the St Lawrence River, Dew came aboard disguised as a pilot. Kendall invited Crippen to meet the pilots as they came aboard. Dew removed his pilot's cap and said: 'Good morning, Dr Crippen. Do you know me? I'm Chief Inspector Dew from Scotland Yard.' After a pause, Crippen replied: 'Thank God it's over. The suspense has been too great. I couldn't stand it any longer.'

LEFT: International coverage followed the spectacular arrest of Crippen. Journalists had travelled to Canada to see Crippen taken from the ship.

end of his journey. Crippen and his secretary were returned to London and tried separately in October 1910 at the Old Bailey. Ethel was judged innocent, but the doctor was found guilty and hanged at Pentonville Prison on 23 November.

Suffragette Riots

The movement for women's equality and rights, especially that of voting, had continued for some 30 years before the great suffragette rally of 21 June 1908 was held in London's Hyde Park. Chartered trains brought women from around the country to hear speakers demand the vote. Some 300,000 protesters carrying 700 banners took part in the Sunday procession through London. Leaders of the movement included Emmeline Pankhurst and her daughters, Christabel and Sylvia. Their Women's Political and Social Union (WPSU) attracted members who supported direct action.

LEFT: Police were forced to arrest many suffragettes on London's streets. This was a delicate action since the offenders were often from the best homes. Men were also arrested during suffragette marches.

ABOVE: Emily Davison was fatally injured at the 1913 Epsom Derby when she ran in front of the King's horse to attach a scarf to its bridle. This was probably not a suicide attempt, as she had a return train ticket from Epsom.

That same year, one of the more militant suffragettes, Edith New, along with Flora Drummond, chained themselves to railings outside 10 Downing Street, yelling 'Votes for women!' Later that year, Edith returned to the Prime Minister's house to throw rocks and break windows. The movement's protests gradually became violent, and by 1910 the arrests were growing.

On 18 November that year, a mass rally in Parliament Square deteriorated into battles between protesters and the police. The women also broke shop windows on Oxford and Regent streets. The event became known as Black Friday, with those arrested given the choice of paying a fine or being imprisoned. Almost all chose incarceration because it helped publicize their cause. When they were jailed in Holloway Prison, the suffragettes demanded to be called political prisoners. Denied this, they began hunger strikes and were force-fed raw eggs through a funnel and tube. This began to shift public opinion in support of their cause.

The worst individual protest was yet to come. On 4 June 1913, Emily Davison, a WPSU member, threw herself in front of the King's horse during a race at the Epsom Derby and was killed. Her funeral drew about 6000 women to St George's Church in the Bloomsbury area of the city. Protests virtually stopped when World

War I began the next year. Women pitched in to do men's jobs, gaining more public respect, and in 1918 the vote was given to women over the age of 30; in 1928 the voting age for women was lowered to 21.

Brides in the Bath

George Joseph Smith was a bigamist who murdered three of his wives in their baths. He had been born in London's East End and served seven years in reform school for thieving from the age of nine. He was legally married in 1898 to Caroline Thornhill, who was jailed for three months after Smith made her steal from her employers. He served two years in prison for the crime, and she left him, moving to Canada, but they were never divorced.

His first victim was Bessie Mundi, whom he met in Bristol in the summer of 1910. She had inherited £2500, and Smith, using the alias of Henry Williams, wed her a few weeks later. In May 1912, they settled in Herne Bay, Kent, and Smith had her make a will with him as the beneficiary. He took her to the doctor after convincing her she suffered from epileptic fits that she couldn't remember. The next day, 13 July, he reported that she had died in her bath. An inquest decided she had had a fit. (Smith had sent her to buy the bath and after her death he returned it.)

In September 1913, Smith met a young nurse, Alice Burnham, in Southampton. They wed on 4 November, the same day he took her for a medical exam in order to take out a life insurance policy again with him as beneficiary. They had a delayed honeymoon in Blackpool, and Smith took her to the doctor for bad headaches. She was found dead in her hotel bath on 12 December. Next, he used the name John Lloyd to court Margaret Lofty. They wed on 18 December 1914. As before, she took out life insurance and on their honeymoon in Highgate, London, he took her to the doctor for headaches. The next day she too died in the bath.

None of the deaths were ruled as suspicious, as no marks were found on the bodies. However, the father of Alice Burnham read the stories about Lofty's death, noted the similarities and informed police. Smith was arrested in February 1915. The bodies were exhumed, but police found no evidence of violence, poison or drugs. However, the Home Office pathologist, Bernard Spilsbury, noted that Bessie Mundy was still clutching a bar of soap and said her hand would have opened during a fit or when fainting.

How did they drown without signs of a struggle? Spilsbury believed Smith had pulled hard on his wives' legs in the bath, and the sudden shock of water caused them to faint. He demonstrated this theory with a female police officer

'They began hunger strikes and were force-fed raw eggs through a funnel and tube.'

ABOVE: Londoners were riveted by George Joseph Smith's murders and how his guilt was exposed by a forensic scientist. *The Daily Mirror* gave his sentencing more importance than the wartime sinking of a liner by the Germans.

wearing a bathing suit who fainted when he jerked her under water and required artificial respiration to recover. Another theory by Smith's barrister was that he had hypnotized them.

Newspapers headlined the 'Brides in the Bath' murders during his trial, which was attended by his real wife, Caroline Thornhill. The jury took 22 minutes to find Smith guilty. The day after he was hanged on 13 August 1915, Caroline married a Canadian soldier.

The Blitz

The Luftwaffe, Germany's air force, began bombing Britain during World War II on 10 July 1940, concentrating on military centres such as ports, radar stations and air bases. By 8 August, nearly 1500 enemy aircraft were conducting bombing raids, paving the way for a land invasion. By September, however, RAF fighters, especially Spitfires and Hurricanes, had won the 'Battle of Britain' in the air, shooting down 1887 German aircraft while losing 1023. The Germans now shifted to night raids on industrial centres in 16 cities, targeting London, Coventry, Sheffield, Southampton and Liverpool, among others.

The Luftwaffe's assault on the capital city began on 7 September 1940 when 300 bombers dropped 370 tons of bombs, killing 448 civilians. The

OPPOSITE: Despite the fury of the Blitz, Londoners stood firm. In 1945, Winston Churchill recalled, 'This Blitz was borne without a word of complaint or the slightest sign of flinching,' and it 'proved London could take it.'

'St Paul's survived to become a symbol of London's resolve and resilience.'

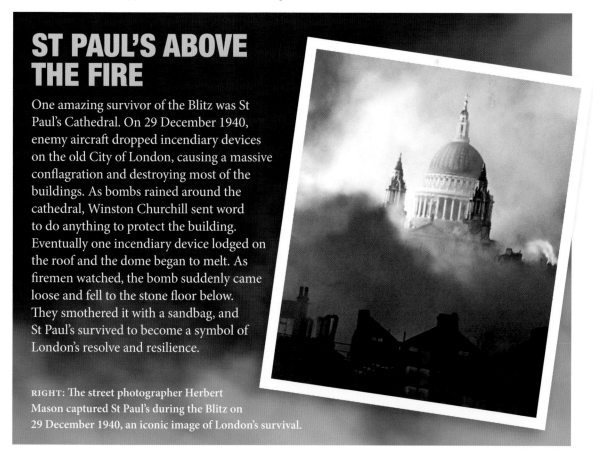

ST PAUL'S ABOVE THE FIRE

One amazing survivor of the Blitz was St Paul's Cathedral. On 29 December 1940, enemy aircraft dropped incendiary devices on the old City of London, causing a massive conflagration and destroying most of the buildings. As bombs rained around the cathedral, Winston Churchill sent word to do anything to protect the building. Eventually one incendiary device lodged on the roof and the dome began to melt. As firemen watched, the bomb suddenly came loose and fell to the stone floor below. They smothered it with a sandbag, and St Paul's survived to become a symbol of London's resolve and resilience.

RIGHT: The street photographer Herbert Mason captured St Paul's during the Blitz on 29 December 1940, an iconic image of London's survival.

attacks continued for 56 consecutive nights and sporadically until 16 May 1941. Londoners withstood the terror and even adopted the German term of 'blitzkrieg' ('lightning war'), shortening it in British fashion to 'the Blitz.' Residents took refuge in private bomb shelters, public air-raid shelters and underground stations, while teams of spotters and firefighters braved the terror from the skies. Many families sent their children for extended country stays with relatives or hosting families. During the war, more than 2 million children were evacuated from London and other vulnerable cities. Other evacuees included mothers, pregnant women, pensioners and hospital patients. The people left in cities observed blackout regulations at night, covering any light that could attract bombers. Those staying on included King George VI and Queen Mary, who visited areas in East London to give moral support to those enduring the destruction. Their own home in Buckingham Palace and its grounds were hit 16 times during the raids, but suffered no casualties and little physical damage, although many windows were blown out.

When the Blitz came to an end, some 30,000 Londoners were dead and about 50,000 injured.

BELOW: John Christie's fatal mistake was to move out of the house where he had buried bodies. He was the key witness against his innocent neighbour, Timothy Evans. When police caught up with him, Christie was homeless.

John Christie

In the space of one decade, John Christie, a World War I veteran, murdered at least eight females, one being a baby, and his wife, Ethel, at his flat at 10 Rillington Place in Notting Hill. After he moved out in 1953, three bodies were discovered in a kitchen alcove and his wife's under the floorboards. Two more were buried in the back garden where a human femur propped up a fence. Five victims were prostitutes who had been raped and strangled, and two were the wife and child of his neighbour, Timothy Evans, who had been charged in 1950 with their murders. In fact Christie was a prosecution witness at his trial, and Evans was hanged – a wrongful conviction that helped abolish capital punishment in Britain in 1965. The following year Evans was posthumously exonerated.

> **'Three bodies were discovered in a kitchen alcove and his wife's under the floorboards.'**

Finally caught, Christie was tried for the death of his wife. He took the witness stand and confessed, 'Yes, I did kill this victim. I killed six others as well over a

period of 10 years.' His defence pleaded guilty by insanity, with his lawyer stating Christie was 'as mad as a March hare.' On 15 June, however, he was sentenced to hang, which took place on 15 July at Pentonville Prison.

Christie's house was torn down and the street rebuilt in the 1970s, renamed Bartle Road.

The Profumo Scandal

The British Secretary State for War, John Profumo, became involved in a sex scandal and intelligence affair in the early 1960s that eventually brought down the Conservative government of Prime Minister Harold Macmillan.

On 8 July 1961, while attending a party at Cliveden House, Lord Astor's country estate, Profumo met Christine Keeler, a 19-year-old dancer and call girl. The introduction was made by Stephen Ward, an osteopath who had links with criminal figures. Also attending was Christine's lover, the Soviet naval attaché Yergeny 'Eugene' Ivanov. Profumo and Keeler became sexually involved, and rumours began to spread about their affair and worries about the Russian connection, this being the height of the Cold War. Ivanov returned to Russia, and Profumo addressed the affair in the House of Commons on 22 March 1963, saying there was 'no impropriety whatsoever.' Too much evidence existed, however, and on 5 June he resigned, apologizing to fellow members. In October, Macmillan resigned.

OPPOSITE: The society osteopath Stephen Ward introduced Christine Keeler (to his right) to the Tory Minister John Profumo. Andrew Lloyd Webber turned his life into a musical, *Stephen Ward*, that opened in 2013 in London.

LEFT: John Profumo, known as Jack, had his political career wrecked by the affair. He was married to the film star Valerie Hobson, who stood by him during the scandal and helped with his later charity work.

Ward was tried for living on immoral earnings and took an overdose of sleeping tablets on 31 July 1963, his last day in court. The jury found him guilty while he was in hospital, and he died on 3 August. Profumo turned his hand to charity work in London's East End and for this was named a Commander of the British Empire (C.B.E.) in 1975. He died at the age of 92 in 2006. Five years earlier in 2001, Keeler published her autobiography, *The Truth at Last: My Story*.

The Kray Twins

Once labelled the most dangerous men in Britain, the Kray twins, Reggie and Ronnie, ruled London's underworld in the 1960s. Growing up in Bethnal Green in East London, they were in gangs as teenagers and even imprisoned for a few days in the Tower of London for failing to report for National Service, being two of the last inmates ever held there. In the 1950s, they took up boxing, but soon formed their own gang called The Firm. Beginning with protection rackets, robberies and buying a snooker club, they graduated to owning several upmarket nightclubs that attracted celebrities, including Judy Garland. Reggie had the charm of a businessman, while Ronnie was rougher. Both were bisexual, and Ronnie was known as 'the Queen Mother' on the gay scene.

By the 1960s their gangster pursuits became heavy-handed. In 1966, they helped Frank 'The Mad Axeman' Mitchell escape from Dartmoor Prison, but then apparently had him killed when he became uncontrollable. Also that year, Ronnie walked into a pub and killed a rival gangster, George Cornell, shooting him in the head. Together in 1967, they murdered another gangster, Jack 'The Hat,' McVitie, luring him to a party in a basement flat, then clearing out the women while Ronnie held him down and Reggie stabbed him to death with a carving knife.

'Ronnie held him down and Reggie stabbed him to death with a carving knife.'

The Krays were convicted in 1969 of murder and sentenced to life, while 14 members of their gang also received jail terms. The twins were separated, with Ronnie sent to Broadmoor Prison after being diagnosed with schizophrenia. Even incarcerated, the Krays operated a protection service for celebrities, including the bodyguards for Frank Sinatra when he visited Britain.

Ronnie died in 1995 of a heart attack in jail at the age of 61. Reggie was diagnosed with bladder cancer and released on compassionate grounds in 2000, dying eight weeks later in a hotel at the age of 66.

Rock & Roll London

The Swinging '60s and '70s in London unleashed years of unlimited self-expression to 'do your own thing' and 'let it all hang out.' Along with the joys of this new freedom came a downside – the expanding drug culture that would claim victims in the coming years, many of them being world-famous musicians. Among those who died were:

Jimi Hendrix

A famed American guitarist, singer and composer, he became one of the most influential musicians of his era, mixing the sounds of rock, blues, jazz and soul. He went to London in 1966 and became a sensation there. He died aged 27 on 18 September 1970 in his Notting Hill flat from an overdose of barbiturates mixed with alcohol.

Keith Moon

The celebrated original drummer for The Who is considered one of the best in the history of rock. He led a wild life and was a notorious jester nicknamed 'Moon the Loon.' He died at the age of 32 on 7 September 1978 in his flat at Curzon Place in Mayfair from an overdose of a drug prescribed to prevent alcoholism. (Four years earlier on 4 July, the American singer, Mama Cass Elliot of The Mamas and the Papas, died at the same age, 32, in the same flat while asleep, apparently of a heart attack.)

Amy Winehouse

An internationally famed British singer and songwriter, Winehouse won many international awards for her songs that transitioned effortlessly between jazz, soul, and rhythm and blues. The press gave extensive coverage of her drug, alcohol and mental health problems, and she died at the age of 27 from alcohol poisoning at her home in the London borough of Camden on 23 July 2011.

RIGHT: Although she led a fragile life with drugs and alcohol, Amy Winehouse's death at the young age of 27 was a shock. Her last recording, a duet with Tony Bennett, was released two months after her death.

Lord Lucan

On 7 November 1974, Sandra Rivett, 29, the nanny of Lord Lucan's children, was bludgeoned to death with a piece of lead piping in the family home at 46 Lower Belgrave Street in West London's expensive Belgravia district. She had gone to the basement to brew a cup of tea. His estranged wife, Veronica, Lady Lucan, went to investigate and was also attacked, running covered in blood from the house to a nearby pub. She had earlier recognized her husband in the house and, although she didn't see him attacking the nanny, named him as the murderer. Lucan had apparently attacked the nanny by mistake, believing her to be his wife, with whom he'd fought over custody of their children.

Lord Lucan, born Richard John Bingham, disappeared immediately. The police investigation found that he had driven to a friend's home in East Sussex to write two letters. After that, the trail went stone cold. The borrowed car he drove was found in Newhaven with bloodstains inside. Some believed he took his own life, drowning from a powerboat he kept there, but more felt he had escaped with the help of powerful friends. He knew

A POISONED UMBRELLA

On 7 September 1978, Georgi Markov was walking on a crowded pavement at lunchtime approaching his bus stop on the south side of Waterloo Bridge. He suddenly felt a sting in his right thigh and turned to see a man pick up a dropped umbrella. The stranger apologized quietly and stepped into a taxi. Markov, 49, soon developed a fever and died four days after the attack. Before dying, he said he believed the man was a Communist agent and the umbrella contained poison. The post mortem examination found a pellet of highly toxic ricin under his skin.

Markov, a 49-year-old Bulgarian who had defected in 1969, was a dissident journalist working for the BBC. He had been a successful novelist and dramatist. In the years following the breakup of the Soviet Union, former KGB officers stated that his assassination had been a joint effort by the Soviet and Bulgarian secret services. In 1992, a former Bulgarian intelligence chief was jailed for 16 months for destroying material related to the murder. Nobody ever faced justice, and Bulgaria officially closed the case in 2013.

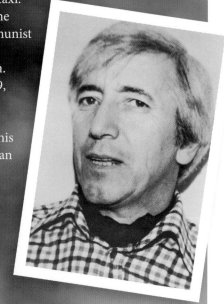

RIGHT: UK doctors and scientists were able to identify the ricin poison that killed Markov because the injected pellet failed to dissolve.

many aristocrats and was a professional gambler, known as 'Lucky Lucan,' who frequented many of London's exclusive clubs.

His disappearance remains one of Britain's greatest unsolved mysteries and a national obsession. Through the years, he has supposedly been sighted in Australia, Paraguay, Mozambique, Goa and a number of other countries. In February 2016 he was declared legally dead, allowing his son, George Bingham, 49, who believes his father is innocent, to inherit his title as the 8th Earl Lucan. Lady Lucan, 78 in 2016, still lives in Belgravia.

Serial Killer and Necrophiliac

From 1978 to 1983, Dennis Nilsen, a civil servant, murdered at least 15 men in London. Born in Scotland, he served as a cook in the army before working in a job centre in north London. He would meet men in pubs who were homeless or homosexual, sometimes working as prostitutes. He invited them to his flat and murdered them, usually strangling them with his tie or drowning them. Then he would keep the corpses in his bed or a chair for a while before cutting them up.

Nilsen murdered at least 12 victims at 195 Melrose Gardens in Willesden Green in northwest London, burying their bodies in his garden. In 1981, he moved to Cranley Gardens at Muswell Hill, north London, and murdered at least three more. After killing them, he would dissect the bodies and boil their heads in a large cooking pot to remove their brains. He cut up the rest of their bodies and stored them in plastic bags in wardrobes in his one-bedroom attic flat. When

BELOW: Dennis Nilsen revealed in 2015 at the age of 70 that he has written and hidden his autobiography that he wants published 'possibly after I'm dead and gone.' He said it comprises thousands of typewritten pages.

GOD'S BANKER

Roberto Calvi, a leading Italian banker, was found hanging from scaffolding below Blackfriars Bridge in London on 19 June 1982. He had five bricks in his pocket and about $14,000 in three different currencies. Known as 'God's Banker' because he had links with the Vatican's bank, Calvi had been missing for nine days before a passer-by discovered his body. An inquest jury ruled his death a suicide. Calvi had tried to kill himself the previous year in jail after being found guilty of illegally exporting several billion lire from Banco Ambrosiano, where he was chairman. Sentenced to four years in prison and released during his appeal, he fled to Venice, shaved off his moustache and flew in a private plane to London. The day before he died, his secretary committed suicide, jumping to her death off his bank, leaving a note about the damage he had done to the employees and the business.

A second inquest in 1983 changed the suicide ruling to an open verdict, and in 2002 Italian forensic scientists concluded he had been murdered. His hands had not touched the bricks and his neck showed no indication of hanging. In 2005, five people associated with Calvi were tried in Rome for his murder and in 2007 were declared innocent.

RIGHT: The forensic scientists' conclusion that Calvi was murdered was an independent report commissioned by his son, Carlo, a former banker.

the stench of the decomposing flesh became too much, he flushed parts down the toilet and drains. In 1983, Nilsen had the nerve to complain about the blocked pipes to his landlord, asking for a waste company to fix them. They discovered the human parts and he was arrested, confessing to 15 or 16 murders.

Nilsen later told police, 'It amazes me that I have no tears for these victims. I have no tears for myself or for those bereaved by my actions.' He was sentenced on 4 November 1983 to life imprisonment with no prospect of parole for 25 years; this was replaced by a whole life tariff in December 1994.

IRA Causes Carnage in London

From the 1970s through to the 1990s, the Irish Republican Army (IRA) set off bombs that killed and wounded Londoners across the city, including the Docklands in the east and Harrods famous store in the west. Two of the most audacious attacks were on prime ministers. Margaret Thatcher and other government ministers survived a bomb on 12 October 1984 at a hotel in Brighton during the Conservative Party Conference. Five people died and 34 were injured. On 7 February 1991, the IRA launched three homemade mortar attacks on 10 Downing Street as John Major met with his cabinet inside. One exploded in the back garden, and three people were slightly wounded.

The atrocity that caused the most carnage came from two bombs that exploded on 20 July 1982 at Hyde Park and Regent's Park. Eleven soldiers were killed and about 40 people injured.

About 10:40 a.m., the mounted Royal Household Cavalry were on the way from their barracks in Knightsbridge to Buckingham Palace for the Changing of the Guard ceremony when a remote-controlled nail bomb exploded in a parked car, killing three soldiers outright and another days later. In total 23 soldiers were injured and seven horses were killed, either from the blast or being destroyed afterwards because of their injuries. One named Sefton received 34 injuries, but survived to become a symbol of resistance and hope, living until 1993.

Less than two hours later, another bomb went off under the bandstand in Regent's Park while the Royal Green Jackets were giving a lunchtime concert for about 120 people. Seven soldiers were killed. The bomb had apparently been left two weeks before and timed for the concert.

In 1987, a Northern Ireland electrician, Gilbert 'Danny' McNamee, was tried for making the Hyde Park bomb and sentenced to 25 years. He was released after 12 because of the Good Friday peace agreement and his conviction was quashed. Another man, John Downey, was arrested in 2013, also for involvement in the Hyde Park bombing, but walked free the next year because police had wrongly sent him a letter in 2007 saying he was not wanted for the crime.

On 17 December 1983, seven months after the 11 soldiers were killed, an IRA car bomb exploded outside London's world famous Harrods department store, killing three police and three civilians and injuring 90 more. Most of the victims were Christmas shoppers. A week earlier, another IRA bomb in London had wounded three soldiers at the Royal Artillery Barracks. A memorial service for the Harrods victims was held on 17 December 2013, the 30th anniversary, and their names are inscribed on two marble plaques at the store.

OPPOSITE: Wreckage strewn in the side street was from Harrods, the Austin car used for the bombing and included shoppers' Christmas gifts. Harrods reopened three days later, vowing that terrorism would not defeat it.

BELOW: Carnage littered the street in Hyde Park after the IRA bomb placed in a Morris car exploded, catching guardsmen in their procession. This was one of the worst IRA atrocities in Britain and a dreadful scene of terrorism.

Britain's Largest Gold Robbery

Six armed robbers wearing balaclavas got lucky on 26 November 1983 when they entered a warehouse at London's Heathrow Airport. They were expecting to steal £3 million in cash from the Brink's-Mat security company. Instead they found 7000 gold bars in 70 cardboard boxes worth around £26 million (£80 million in today's money). Their access had been easy because a security guard had tipped them off about the cash and even opened the warehouse door for them and pointed out the two guards who had keys and combinations to a vault and three safes.

Getting the gold out was the problem. The robbers brought in a van to handle the more than three tonnes of bullion. As they left, they even wished the bound security guards a happy Christmas. Their real difficulty was selling the gold. Since it was too risky to offer pure gold, the gang had other criminals smelt it with copper and brass. Some £13 million was disposed of in this way.

Police suspected an inside job and traced the crime to the security guard who quickly named the robbers. When Detective Constable John Fordham began looking in the garden of one suspect, Kenneth Noye, the man stabbed him to death. Noye was found innocent on grounds of self-defence, but police soon found 11 gold bars at his place. He received a 14-year sentence and was released in 1994 after seven. Two years later, he killed a motorist in a road-rage incident and is now serving a life sentence.

'At least £10 million in gold is thought to be still buried in gardens.'

Only two of the robbers were convicted, but it has been estimated that over 20 people connected to the heist have been murdered after underworld disputes. At least £10 million in gold is thought to be still buried in gardens, farmyards and other unknown locations.

More Heathrow Robberies

On 11 February 2002, two robbers dressed as policemen approached a British Airways' plane from Bahrain. They overpowered a worker who was unloading currencies and escaped with £4.6 million. The unknown criminals were never caught and none of the stolen money was recovered.

On 19 March 2002, armed men stole £2.6 million in US dollars from a van parked in a secure area near the terminal building after pulling a knife on the driver and tying him up. The money had been loaded off a flight from Bahrain into a British Airways' van. The robbers transferred it to another B.A. vehicle that was later found burned out in Feltham, west London. Police arrested 12 suspects in May – five were found guilty and sentenced to a total of 25 years. One was the insider driver who had claimed to be a victim.

On 6 February 2004, another robbery of a Heathrow warehouse followed a similar pattern of the great gold robbery. An insider let four robbers into the Menzies World Cargo warehouse to steal £1.75 million in cash. He was arrested and later identified the criminals. He was sentenced to six years in 2007, but released the same year and now lives with his family with new names in a secret location. The four robbers were jailed for between 15 years and life in the first British trial in 400 years before a judge and no jury.

On 18 May 2004, eight robbers attempted to steal £33 million in cash, gold and gems after an insider tipped them off about the holdings. They used a van to

smash into the Swissport warehouse and threatened guards and staff with hockey sticks and batons. However, police had been observing their earlier activities, and more than 100 armed officers moved in as the gang was loading boxes of gold into the van. They were given sentences of up to 13 years.

Poll Tax Riots

The Conservative government of Prime Minister Margaret Thatcher passed a new tax called the community charge in 1989, which was to replace the property rates system. It went into effect that year in Scotland and a year later in England and Wales. Popularly known as the poll tax, this shifted the tax burden from the rich to the poor, since every adult would pay a flat rate instead of paying more for larger, expensive houses in better parts of the country. Some 38 million people would have to pay the new individual tax against 14 million who paid house rates. The Secretary of State for the Environment, Nicholas Ridley, summed it up: 'A duke would pay the same as a dustman.'

Many protests were held throughout Britain. On 31 March 1990, a rally against the tax by some 200,000 demonstrators took place in central London, resulting in a riot that injured 113 people, including 45 police officers. Bottles, bricks and other missiles were thrown at police and their vans and a 20-strong team of mounted police became targets as they rounded on crowds in Trafalgar Square. The violence died down about 3 a.m. the next day after 491 arrests and considerable damage to property.

Thatcher remained a fervent supporter of the tax despite continued unrest and

ABOVE: Vans have been the preferred means of robbery at Heathrow. The Brink's-Mat gang brought their own and one was used to smash into the Swissport warehouse. Other robbers simply stole airport vans to convey stolen goods.

the refusal of many individuals to pay. By August, 27 per cent of Londoners had not paid. Convinced that her actions were causing great political damage, leaders in her party forced her resignation in November. Her successor, John Major, repealed the tax, replacing it in 1992 with the council tax system that is still in effect today.

Other Modern Riots in London

In **1981**, tensions between black residents and police in Brixton, south London, had been building after a new law designed to reduce street crime allowed police to stop and search people. More than 1000 had been stopped in six days, and residents believed that a disproportionate number of black people were being targeted by police. After news spread of an arrest, riots exploded from 8 to 10 April, with more than 300 people injured and 145 buildings damaged at an estimated cost of £7.5 million. That summer, the city also saw disturbances break out in about 20 other locations.

In **1985**, police raided a home on 28 September, again in Brixton, looking for a burglary suspect and accidentally shot the man's mother, Cherry Groce, in her bed. Street violence soon broke out with rioters petrol-bombing cars and looting shops. As the violence spread, Police Constable Keith Blakelock was called to protect firefighters at the Broadwater Farm estate in Tottenham, north London. A gang surrounded him and attacked with knives and machetes, killing him. His murder is still unsolved. Some 50 people were injured during the riots and 200 arrested. Cherry Groce was crippled and hospitalized for two years. The officer who shot her was cleared of criminal charges in 1987.

In **2011**, armed police stopped a minicab on 4 August in Tottenham, north London, and ordered Mark Duggan, 29, out. The Metropolitan Police's anti-drug task force said it had evidence that Duggan, from the Broadwater Farm estate in Tottenham, was involved in drug trafficking and gun crimes. One officer, believing he saw a gun in Duggan's hand, fired twice and killed him. An unfired pistol was recovered nearby wrapped in a sock. This tragic event set off riots and looting around the city until 8 August. Petrol bombs were thrown at police, two police cars set alight and a double-decker bus burned out. Shops and houses suffered millions of pounds in damage. By 15 August, more than 2000 people had been arrested. The disorder and violence also spread for six days to other British cities, including Birmingham, Manchester, Liverpool, Nottingham and Bristol. Across the country, five people died, 3000 were arrested and the property damage was estimated at some £200 million. In 2014, a jury ruled that Duggan had been lawfully killed.

OPPOSITE: Many among the London police lacked shields and other riot gear as they encountered violent poll tax rioters. Officers used horse charges and containment lines, but were outnumbered by the demonstrators,who attacked shops and cars.

ABOVE: Large riots resulted from the police shooting death of Mark Duggan in Tottenham, north London, on 4 August 2011. The police were part of Operation Trident dealing with gun crimes in London's African and Caribbean communities.

Stephen Lawrence

On 22 April 1993, Stephen Lawrence, an 18-year-old black man, was surrounded and stabbed to death by a racist white gang as he waited with a friend for a bus in Eltham, southeast London. Stephen was a gifted student who planned to be an architect. The slow actions of the police in investigating and arresting those guilty of the crime led to criticisms of racism within the force and brought in changes to eliminate such attitudes.

'The government conducted a public enquiry into the police handling of the case.'

In May 1993, South Africa's Nelson Mandela met with Stephen's parents and expressed concern over the case. That same month, police arrested five youths and charged two with murder, but the charges were dropped after it was decided the witness who had identified them was unreliable. Stephen's parents, Doreen and Neville Lawrence, launched a private prosecution in 1994 but it failed for the same reason, despite a covert video shot in the flat of one suspect, Gary Dobson, showing four suspects using racist language and violently brandishing knives.

An inquest in 1997 ruled Stephen's death an unlawful killing 'in a completely unprovoked racist attacks by five youths.' The following year, the government conducted a public inquiry into the police handling of the case, and Police Commissioner Sir Paul Condon apologized to the Lawrence family, admitting mistakes were made. In 1999, an official report by Sir William Macpherson accused the police of institutional racism and made 70 recommendations for improving racial attitudes. Another report in 2009 said police had made significant progress to combat its racism.

ABOVE: Gary Dobson (left) and David Norris (right) were found guilty of Stephen Lawrence's murder, but it took 18 years before they were convicted by DNA evidence. The case remains open.

In 2010, one of the murder suspects, Gary Dobson, began a five-year sentence for trafficking £350,000 worth of cannabis. On 14 November 2011, he and David Norris went on trial for killing Stephen and on 3 January 2012 were found guilty, based on Stephen's DNA found on their clothes. Both received life sentences. Other suspects are still being sought, such as Jamie Acourt who is believed to be on the run in Spain. In March 2016, police released an enhanced CCTV image of a possible witness near the crime scene.

Doreen Lawrence opened a £10 million architectural centre in 2008 to honour her son. Located in Deptford in southeast London, it was established to improve opportunities for disadvantaged young people.

Death on the Doorstep

Jill Dando was one of Britain's most beloved television presenters and journalists. Employed by the BBC, she co-presented Crimewatch, a television show that depicted real crimes and asked the public for help if they had any information relating to the cases.

On 26 April 1999, a man walked up while Dando was unlocking her front door at about 11:32 a.m. at her home in Fulham, west London. Grabbing her from behind, he forced her down and shot her dead with a single bullet to the head. He then walked down her residential street and disappeared. Only one neighbour saw the white man who was aged around 40.

Speculation said this was revenge by a criminal or criminals that her programme had put behind bars. Her murder appeared to be a professional hit with no clues left behind. Another theory suggested it had been a Serbian hitman because weeks before Dando had fronted an appeal for Kosovan-Albanian refugees.

In May 2000, police arrested Barry George who lived about a half-mile from Dando. He was known to stalk women as they walked home and had taken thousands of pictures of them. He was found guilty in July and sentenced to life imprisonment. The only direct evidence against him was a speck of firearm residue deep in the pocket of his coat. This was discredited during an appeal hearing, and George, 48, was cleared of the murder on 1 August 2008 at a retrial as there had never been a weapon found, witnesses to the murder or a motive. He was not awarded compensation for his eight years in jail because the trial did not show 'beyond a reasonable doubt' that he did not commit the offence. The Dando case remains open.

ABOVE: The murder of Jill Dando remains unsolved. That Monday morning, she was returning from a weekend at the home of her fiancé, Dr Alan Farthing, in Chiswick, London.

ABOVE: Thirteen people died on a number 30 double-decker bus at Tavistock Square when the fourth and final bomb exploded. The driver, George Psaradakis, helped the injured, saying he was shocked and overwhelmed by their conditions.

RIGHT: A man assists a wounded woman from the Edgware Road tube station after that attack. Doctors and pedestrians rushed to aid those injured and traumatized. A total of 497 survivors related their experiences at the coroner's inquests.

Terrorist Bombings of 2005

In the worst single terrorist attack in Britain, four suicide bombers wearing rucksacks packed with explosives killed 52 people and injured hundreds more. The tragic day happened on 7 July 2005 and is often called '7/7.' The previous day, London had been awarded the 2012 Olympics.

Three of the bombs exploded on underground carriages just before 8:50 during the morning commute. All trains had left King's Cross station. The group's leader, Mohammad Sidique Khan, 30, detonated his device at the Edgware Road station, killing six passengers. Shehzad Tanweer, 22, detonated his between Liverpool and Aldgate stations, killing seven. The last and most deadly bomb was carried by Germaine Lindsay and exploded as it left King's Cross station, killing 26.

'A permanent memorial of 52 steel pillars was unveiled on 7 July 2009 in Hyde Park.'

After these atrocities, Hasib Hussain, 18, detonated his bomb about an hour later on a number 30 double-decker bus at Tavistock Square, killing 13 people. This occurred in front of the headquarters of the British Medical Association, and dozens of doctors rushed to perform lifesaving acts.

A permanent memorial of 52 steel pillars was unveiled on 7 July 2009 in Hyde Park to remember the victims, whose names are listed on a separate plaque.

Lee Rigby

One of London's most shocking terrorist killings occurred on 22 May 2013 when a serving British soldier, Lee Rigby, was confronted and killed in a frenzied attack with knives and a cleaver on a street in Woolwich near his barracks and a school. Rigby was a seven-year veteran who had served in Afghanistan. His brutal death was recorded on video and shown on television. The murderers were Islamic fanatics, Michael Adebolajo, 28, and Michael Adebowale, 22, who first ran Rigby down with a car. After killing him, they beheaded him in front of pedestrians and one ranted that it was because Muslims were being killed daily by British soldiers. He added, 'You and your kids will be next.' They did not flee, instead posing for

BELOW: A memorial of flowers covered the street where Lee Rigby was killed. His name is also on a plaque in St George's Chapel near his barracks with those of 10 other service personnel and civilians from the area.

pictures. One also gave a bystander a two-page note stating his reasons for the attack. A brave onlooker, Ingrid Loyau-Kennett, was so outraged, she walked up to the assailant who was holding a knife and asked him to hand over his weapons. When he told her they wanted to start a war in London, she said, 'You're going to lose. It's only you versus many.' Arriving on the scene, police shot and wounded the two who were charging at them. Tried and convicted on 26 February 2014, the terrorists were both sentenced to life in prison.

'His brutal death was recorded on video and shown on television.'

Radioactive Assassination

Alexander Litvinenko, a former Russian spy who fled to London to become a fierce critic of the Kremlin, was killed in 2006 with radioactive polonium-210 at the age of 44. The poison had apparently been added to his cup of tea by another former Russian agent.

Litvinenko had been an officer with the Federal Security Service (FSB) that replaced the old spy organization, the KGB, which he had joined in 1988. He fled to London in 2000 to work for MI6, the British secret service, and six years later became a British citizen. At London's Millennium Hotel on 1 November 2006, he had green tea with two former Russian spies, Andrei Lugovoi and Dmitri

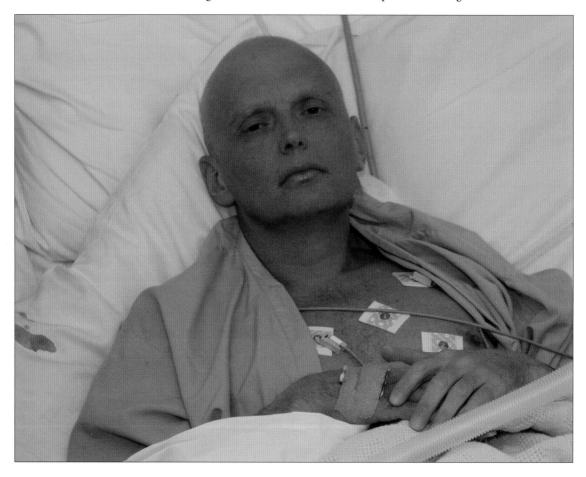

Kovtun. That evening he became ill and three days later he was admitted to Barnet General Hospital in north London. On 17 November, he became worse and was transferred to University College Hospital, central London, dying six days later. He told police, 'I knew they wanted to kill me, actually.'

According to his widow, Maria, as he lay dying, Litvinenko blamed Russian President Vladimir Putin for the poisoning. Putin was his boss at the KGB, and they had argued when Litvinenko complained about corruption in the agency. Litvinenko was arrested in 1998 for exposing a plot to kill a Russian tycoon and left the service when acquitted after nine months in jail.

In 2007, Britain's director of public prosecutions ruled that Andrei Lugovoi should be charged with the assassination, but Russia refused to extradite him. An inquiry set up by the British government decided in January 2015 that the murder had probably been approved by Putin.

> **'As he lay dying, Litvinenko blamed Russian President Vladimir Putin.'**

The Hatton Garden Heist

Britain's largest ever burglary took place between 2 and 5 April 2015, an Easter weekend, when a gang of between four to six men broke into the Hatton Garden Safe Deposit vault in the London borough of Camden. Jewellers used the vault for storage, and the raiders stole some £14 million in gems, cash and other valuables. Considerable effort and ingenuity were required to crack the vault. The gang bored a small hole through a concrete wall to bypass the reinforced metal doors, then forced open 72 of the 999 safe deposit boxes. An alarm went off while they worked, but was ignored by police. They became aware of the burglary on 7 April but found no forced entry outside the building. The gang had disabled a lift and climbed down its shaft to the vault in the basement.

Police combed through thousands of hours of CCTV footage and gathered other evidence, such as DNA, fingerprints, mobile phone calls and car number plates. The leaders were caught after they boasted in a pub about their raid. Police arrested seven who took part and were surprised at their advanced ages, averaging 63 years. The oldest, Brian Reader, was 76 and travelled to the crime scene on a free pensioner's bus pass. They were described in the press as 'Diamond Geezers' and 'Bad Grandpas.' Scotland Yard's Peter Spindler called them 'analogue criminals operating in a digital world.' One man, known only as Basil, was caught on CCTV in a red-haired wig, but never apprehended.

On 9 March 2016, four of the burglars were sentenced to seven years and one to six years. Some £10 million worth of jewellery has not been recovered, but some items were found buried under gravestones in a cemetery.

London Today

London has seen its problems and violence prolonged by the city's long history and magnified by its leading role in the world. Invasions and the peaceful influx of peoples from the British Empire and Commonwealth brought a richness of cultures that have competed and joined together to resolve their differences. The violent clashes of armies and religions and politics are distant memories of how Britain was built. Monarchs now cut off ribbons instead of heads, and Londoners rush to sales instead of executions. Problems remain, as always, but London's resilience and delightful optimism assure a successful and exciting future for this beloved old city.

OPPOSITE: As Alexander Litvinenko was dying, he, with help, composed a letter to Russia's President Putin saying 'the howl of protest from around the world will reverberate, Mr Putin, in your ears for the rest of your life.'

BIBLIOGRAPHY

Ackroyd, Peter, *Foundation: The History of England from Its Earliest Beginnings to the Tudors* (St. Martin's Griffin, 2013)

Ackroyd, Peter, *The History of England from Henry VIII to Elizabeth I* (St. Martin's Griffin, 2014)

Arnold, Catharine, *The Sexual History of London: From Roman Londinium to the Swinging City – Lust, Vice, and Desire Across the Ages* (St. Martin's Press, 2011)

Balen, Malcolm, *The Secret History of the South Sea Bubble: The World's First Great Financial Scandal* (Harper, 2003)

Barron, Caroline M., *London in the Later Middle Ages: Government and People 1200–1500* (OUP, 2005)

Bingham, Janes, *Tudors* (Arcturus, 2011)

Briggs, Asa, *A Social History of England* (Viking Press, 1983)

Crone, Rosalind, *Violent Victorians: Popular Entertainment in Nineteenth Century London* (Manchester University Press, 2012)

Defoe, Daniel; Backscheider, Paula R. (Ed.), *A Journal of the Plague Year* (W. W. Norton, 1992)

Delderfield, Eric R. (Ed.), *Kings and Queens of England* (Weathervane Books, 1978)

Evans, Eric (Ed.), *British History* (Parragon, 1999)

Flanders, Judith, T*he Victorian City: Everyday Life in Dickens' London* (Thomas Dunne Books, 2014)

Fraser, Antonia, *Cromwell* (Grove Press, 2001)

Gardiner, Juliet, *The Blitz: The British Under Attack* (Harper Press, 2010)

Gascoigne, Bamber, *Encyclopedia of Britain* (Macmillan, 1994)

George, Mary Dorothy, *London Life in the 18th Century* (Chicago Review Press, 2005)

Hanson, Neil, *The Great Fire of London: In That Apocalyptic Year*, 1666 (Wiley, 2002)

Hitchcock, Tim; Shoemaker, Robert, *London Lives: Poverty, Crime and the Making of a Modern City, 1690-1800* (Cambridge University Press, 2015)

Jones, Nigel, *Tower: An Epic History of the Tower of London* (St. Martin's Griffin, 2013)

Linebaugh, Peter, *The London Hanged: Crime and Civil Society in the 18th Century* (Verso, 2006)

Matthews, Michael, *The Riots* (Silvertail Books, 2016)

Mayhew, Henry, *The London Underworld in the Victorian Period: Authentic First-person Accounts by Beggars, Thieves and Prostitutes* (Dover Publications, 2005)

Meyer, G. J., *The Tudors: The Complete History of England's Most Notorious Dynasty* (Bantam, 2011)

Milne, Gustav, *English Heritage Book of Roman London* (B. T. Batsford, 1996)

Mount, Toni, *Everyday Life in Medieval London* (Amberley, 2015)

Norton, Elizabeth, *The Tudor Treasury* (Metro Books, 2014)

Oakley, Malcolm, *East London History: The People, The Places* (CreateSpace Independent Publishing Platform, 2016)

Perring, Dominic, *Roman London* (Routledge, 2014)

Picard, Liza, *Restoration London: Everyday Life in the 1660s* (Weidenfeld & Nicolson History, 2003)

Porter, Stephen, *Shakespeare's London: Everyday Life in London 1580–1616* (Amberley, 2011)

Rumbelow, Donald, *The Complete Jack the Ripper* (Virgin Books, 2013)

Schofield, John, *London 1100–1600: The Archaeology of the Capital City* (Equinox, 2011)

Shesgreen, Sean, *Images of the Outcast: The Urban Poor in the Cries of London from the Sixteenth to the Nineteenth Century* (Manchester University Press, 2002)

Webb, Simon, *Life in Roman London* (The History Press, 2012)

Webb, Simon, *Dynamite, Treason & Plot: Terrorism in Victorian and Edwardian London* (The History Press, 2012)

Weir, Alison, *The Six Wives of Henry VIII* (Grove Press, 1991)

White, Jerry, *A Great and Monstrous Thing: London in the Eighteenth Century* (Harvard University Press, 2013)

White, Jerry, *London in the Nineteenth Century: "A Human Awful Wonder of God"* (Jonathan Cape, 2007)

White, Jerry, *London in the Twentieth Century: A City and Its People* (Random House, 2008)

Wilkes, John, *The London Police in the Nineteenth Century* (Lerner, 1985)

INDEX

PICTURE CREDITS

1 / 2 / 3 / 4 / 5 / 6 / 7 / 8 / 9 / 10 / 11 / 12 / 13 / 14

3 Miles West   2 Miles West   CAMDEN   1 Mile West

1 Mile North

1 Mile South

REGENTS

KENSINGTON GARDENS

H Y D E

SERPENTINE RIVER

P A R K

BROMP

CHELSEA REACH

R

LAMBETH

SOUTH WESTERN
RAILWAY DEPOT

67 / 66 / 65 / 64 / 63 / 62 / 61 / 60 / 59 / 58 / 57 / 56 / 55 / 54

3 Miles West   2 Miles West   1 Mile West

LONDON, PUBLISHED BY C.

EXPLANATION O
City of London .... Red. | Borough of Southwark ... Blue
City & Liberties of Westminster Yellow | Ditto of Marylebone .... Red